The Pere Marquette Revenue FREIGHT CARS

13110 Beverly Park Road
Mukilteo, Washington 98275

Library of Congress Control Number
00-140037

ISBN No.
0-945434-71-5

PUBLISHER
Robert L. Hundman

EDITOR
Sigrid K. Powell

CONTRIBUTING EDITOR
Jeffrey M. Koeller

PRODUCTION ASSISTANT
Sandy Mewhorter

GRAPHICS/PHOTO & DIAGRAM REPRODUCTION
Sigrid K. Powell

Printed in Hong Kong

Revenue
FREIGHT CARS

by Arthur B. Million and John C. Paton

COVER: No car typifies the Pere Marquette more than the 50-foot double-door steel automobile car. PM No. 72000 is an example of the cars built by Greenville Steel Car Company in 1940. She was equipped with a Duryea cushion underframe and a perforated steel interior lining for auto parts shipments. *GSC Photo - John C. Paton Collection*

PAGE i: Pere Marquette's second series of fifty-foot auto cars had wider door openings and lacked the end doors of their predecessors built in 1930. PM No. 71294 was built by Ralston Steel Car Company in October 1936, part of an order for 100 cars in series 71250-71349. *RSC Photo - C&OHS Collection*

THIS PAGE: Brakeman Fred Hess rides the top of the ladder of a Pere Marquette 40' auto car from series 90350-91849 at Saginaw, Michigan, in August 1946. It was common practice for brakemen to ride on top of the car, or on the side ladder, while signaling to be better seen by the engineer or a ground man transferring signals to the engineer. This car and sister No. 90816 in the background were built by Pullman Car & Manufacturing Company in 1930. Both have been shopped and repainted at the Saginaw Shops. *C&OHS Collection*

PAGE iv: Pere Marquette car mechanics inspect and repack journal boxes on a PM 40' auto car at Saginaw, Michigan, in August 1946. This view nicely shows the details of the Hutchins roof with which cars numbered 90350-91849 were delivered. This particular car has Apex metal replacement running boards, and is equipped with Evans Type-E auto loaders and has eight floor tubes (note the "8E" stencil on the door under the white stripe). *C&OHS Collection*

PAGE vi: An operator rides the 15-ton overhead crane at Pere Marquette's Wyoming Shops in Grand Rapids, Michigan. PM No. 31902, a 36' wooden box car with truss rods, was built by Haskell & Barker Car Company in 1904 and is nearing the end of its revenue life in this May 1924 photo. *C&OHS Collection*

Contents

Foreword & Acknowledgements

We first met through correspondence in 1978 when John was the Modeling Editor of the Basement Subdivision of the Chesapeake & Ohio Historical Newsletter, and Art was the Pere Marquette Historian for the C&O Historical Society. We found that we shared some common interests, especially the Pere Marquette and the C&O in Michigan. As our friendship continued to grow, we found that each of us was a wealth of information for the other. Since we both did custom painting of models, John could always supply information for painting them. On the other hand, much of the research for John's BL2 book, *Chesapeake and Ohio BL2 Diesels* (C&OHS, 1991), was done by Art, also a big fan of these locomotives. It was from that collaboration that the idea for this project emerged. We wanted to do something on the PM together, and a book on its freight cars just seemed a natural. It's now four years since that decision, and we are still the very best of friends.

Together, we have tried to provide in this publication all pertinent data concerning Pere Marquette revenue freight cars. While researching this subject, it was found that interest in the PM still remains high, but after nearly fifty years of being a "fallen flag," data is getting harder to find. Maybe this is why the interest level remains so intense.

One area lacking authoritative information for a publication of this type is a record indicating the renumbering of the cars from the predecessor railroads into the PM. While records still survive, such as *Official Railway Equipment Registers*, any attempt to match car types and series would, at best, be speculative and not necessarily an accurate historical record. We recognize this lack of information and apologize for it, but we will not speculate.

What has been saved of Pere Marquette freight car history, and it has been considerable, has been through the efforts of former company personnel, PM railfans, historians, libraries, and outside organizations. We are grateful to all for saving this data and we thank them. We hope that through the efforts of this publication, more information will surface and be forwarded to the Pere Marquette Historical Society, P. O. Box 422, Grand Haven, MI 49417, and that this publication can be updated at a future date.

We would like to acknowledge and thank the following for their assistance:

Richard Burg, Thomas W. Dixon, Jr., Mark A. Kapka, Art Lamport, Keith Retterer, Carl W. Shaver, Philip A. Shuster, Henry Walhout, Al Westerfield, Al Kresse, Gordon Lydeksen, Kent McFaden, the Muskegon Railroad Historical Society, Pat O'Boyle, Wayland Brown, Gil and Kathy Riggs, Jeffrey Koeller, Bob Hundman, Charles Winters, W. C. Whittaker, Al Lonsberry, Ted Luce, Peter Blau, Gail Harris, Anne Hughes, the CSRM Paul Darrell Collection, the Grand Rapids Public Library, Charlotte C. Paton, Roland Radtke, National Archives of Canada, Gay Lepkey, Tom LaMaire, MLM Photo Collection, and Attila Zombor.

-- *Arthur B. Million, John C. Paton*

Dedicated to the memory of Henry J. Walhout

v

Grand Rapids M

Introduction

You can tell a lot about a railroad by a study of its freight cars. More than that, you can tell a lot about the area it serves. Freight cars are reactive objects, in that they reflect conditions rather than create them. The formation and gradual evolution of the Pere Marquette Railway's freight car fleet is a mirror of the economic history of Michigan. Consider first the types of cars. Cars are merely, after all, containers built to transport goods, and the types of cars reflect the types of goods being transported. Of equal importance is the quantity of each type of car, indicating the relative importance of each type of traffic. In 1900, Michigan was primarily rural, with lumbering as its largest basic industry. What manufacturing was done was confined to Detroit and Grand Rapids with its furniture industry. Over the years, manufacturing assumed greater importance with the rise of the automobile industry, and the composition of the Pere Marquette's freight car fleet reflected this. On one hand, the decline of lumbering is reflected in the decline in the number of flat cars. On the other hand, a steady stream of more and bigger box cars, was acquired until they dominated the roster. Not only that, cars specifically designed for automobiles and automobile parts were developed and built. In some cases, these modifications are quite apparent, such as the steel supports for auto frames built into many of the PM's gondolas. Other developments were less visible, because they were confined to the interiors of box cars, such as racks for the loading of automobiles. By the time of its absorption into the Chesapeake & Ohio Railway in 1947, the Pere Marquette possessed a highly specialized fleet of freight cars specifically designed to carry the equally highly specialized goods produced in its area of service.

The purpose of this book is to present a chronological history of those cars, from the pre-Pere Marquette days of its predecessor component lines, up until the Pere Marquette itself was absorbed by the Chesapeake & Ohio. Where we have been able to match car photographs with diagrams, we have done so. Where no photo or diagram exist, we have used what was available. In trying to make the job more manageable, we have arbitrarily divided the 47-year-plus time span into three parts. The Trans-Michigan herald is used for cars built before World War I, the State of Michigan logo is used for cars built from World War I until about 1935, and the familiar Pere Marquette rectangle represents cars of the most modern PM era. Included also are some rebuilt cars from programs started by the Pere Marquette and, in some cases, continued by the C&O after the takeover. Although thousands of Pere Marquette cars were ultimately relettered for the C&O, it's only these few rebuild-program cars lettered C&O that appear in this book.

Finally, a chapter on modeling some of these cars is included. So, too, are lettering diagrams (Appendix B) for accurate lettering information.

A book such as this is an exercise in subtlety, and is not for those who think that if you've seen one box car, you've seen them all. We believe that you haven't seen them all until you really *have* seen them all, and that is what we have attempted to present here: the most comprehensive survey of Pere Marquette freight cars possible, gleaned from every source we could find, plus a few that found us. We hope that our efforts will be of help to freight car historians and modelers, and to all who wish to gain a deeper understanding of what the Pere Marquette Railway was all about.

Articles on the Pere Marquette Railway usually begin by pointing out that it was formed by the amalgamation of several smaller lines in the year 1900. This fact bears more than usual relevance in the case of the PM's freight car fleet, because all of its first revenue freight cars were drawn from the rosters of predecessor roads. The largest of these was the Flint & Pere Marquette, which contributed nearly 4,000 cars to the fleet. The Chicago & West Michigan, next in size, brought with it slightly more than 3,000 cars, while the third major contributor, the Detroit, Grand Rapids & Western, added another 2,200 cars to the roster. Later acquisions, such as the Saginaw, Tuscola & Huron, with about 200 cars, brought the Pere Marquette's freight car roster to approximately 10,000 during its early years. The December 1900 *Equipment Register*, reproduced here, is interesting because is shows that even a full year after the formation of the new railroad, freight cars are still listed separately by the name and number of each predecessor road. Ultimately, most, if not all, of these cars were incorporated into the new Pere Marquette and were relettered and renumbered for the PM; however, no data exists showing which cars received what numbers. Although some educated guessing can be made along these lines, it remains just guessing. No diagrams exist for predecessor road's cars, but photos do, and they are included herein.

(Continued on Page 6)

Official Railway Equipement Register - December 1900

PERE MARQUETTE RAILROAD.

GENERAL OFFICERS.

W. W. Crapo, Chairman of Board...New Bedford, Mass
Chas. M. Heald, President .... Detroit, Mich
Mark T. Cox, Vice President.......... New York, N.Y.
John M. Graham, Vice-President... ..... Boston Mass.
Charles Merriam, Sec. and Treas........ "
Stanford T. Crapo, Gen. Manager.......Detroit, Mich.
Henry C. Potter, Jr., Compt. and Asst. Sec.. "

Arthur Patriarche, Traffic Manager.....Detroit, Mich.
F. V. Davis, Gen. Freight Agent......... ..
P. F. Gaines, Asst. Gen. Freight Agent.... "
H. F. Moeller, Gen. Passenger Agent. ..
J. K. V. Agnew, Supt. Gr.Rapids Dist.,Grand Rapids,Mich.
W. D. Trump, Supt. Saginaw Dist........Saginaw, Mich.
David Crombie, Supt. of Transportation...Detroit, Mich.

Geo. F. Weidman, Supt. of Telegraph....Detroit, Mich
John Doyle, Supt. Tracks............ ... "
W. L. Mercereau, Supt. Steamships..,L. .gton, Mich
B. Haskell, Supt. Motive Power........S. .inaw, Mich
R. D. Norris, Acting Purchasing Agent... "
G. M. Kimball, Chief Engineer...........Detroit, Mich

GENERAL OFFICES, DETROIT, MICH.

Miles of road operated, 1901. Gauge, 3 ft. and 4 ft. 8½ in. Locomotives, 220. American Express Co. operates over this line. Pere Marquette and Pullman Sleeping Cars operate over this line.

Limit of load allowed to pass over this line in excess of marked capacity: In cars less than 40000 lb. capacity, 10 per cent.; in cars 40000 lb. capacity and over, 10 per cent.

FREIGHT EQUIPMENT.

The freight cars of this Company are lettered "Pere Marquette," "F. & P. M. R.R.," "S., T. & H. R.R.," "D., G. R. & W," "D., L. & N.," "G. R., L. & D.," "C. & W. M.," "Stickley Bros. Co.," "S. Kilbourn & Co.," "Wells-Higman Co.," "Elk Rapids Car Co.," "Ballou Basket Works" and are numbered and classified as follows:

F. & P. M. CARS.

Kind of Cars.	Numbers.	Inside Dimensions. Length	Width	Height	Capacity.	No.
Box. ....See Note A.	1 to 299	27,29, 33	8	....	20,30, 40000	146
" 4-wheel............	300 to 399	19	8	6.6	20000	15
" ....See Note B.	400 to 499	33	8	6.9	40000	71
"	500 to 799	35.10	8.5	7.9	60000	250
"	800 to 849	32.6	8.2	6.6	40000	44
"	1800 to 1899	33.2	8.2	6.6	40000	49
"	2000 to 2120	33	8	6.9	40000	111
"	2121 to 2199	29	8	6.6	30000	84
"	2400 to 2799	33	8.2	6.5	40000	344
"	5500 to 5599	32.10	8	6.6	30 & 40000	40
"	6060 to 6099	33	8	6.6	40000	36
"	6100 to 6189	33	8	6.6	50000	81
"	6200 to 6499	33	8	6.8	40000	281
"	6500 to 6699	33.6	8.2	7.4	50000	184
Furniture...............	2800 to 2809	37.5	8	7	40000	9
"	2810 to 2834	37.4	8.6	8	50000	19
"	6190 to 6199	37.6	8.10	8.8	50000	9
"	6700 to 6729	40.8	8.6	5	50000	26
"	6730	49	8.6	....	50000	1
Refrigerator..............	2880 to 2889	27.6	8.4	7.2	50000	10
Stock.....................	900 to 912	33.5	8.4	7.7	40000	12
"	913 to 920	29	8	....	40000	8
" Also See Note B.	921 to 999	33.5	8.4	7.7	40000	4
Charcoal..................	1900 to 1999	33 & 35	8	....	30 & 40000	85
"	2850 to 2864	35	8	8	40000	2
" Also See Note A...	6050 to 6058	35	8	8	40000	4
Flat.. " " "	850 to 899	34 & 36	8	....	40000	3
" ..See Notes A, C and D.	1000 to 1799	34 & 36	8	....	40000	555
"	7000 to 7249	34 & 36	8	....	40 & 50000	222
"	8000 to 8199	34 & 36	8	....	50000	185
" Log	6000 to 6049	22	10	....	40000	18
" "	7250 to 7299	22	10	....	40000	19
"	16400 to 16449	36	8.6	....	60000	50
Coal......................	4000 to 4199	32.4	8	....	40000	170
" ....See Note C.	4200 to 4299	33	8	....	40000	26
"	4300 to 4399	33 & 35	8	....	40000	22
" (Drop Bottom).	9000 to 9100	35	....	....	50000	100
" Pere Marquette	9101 to 9300	35	....	....	60000	200
Charcoal............Note A.	162, 194, 1123	33 & 35	8	....	20,30, 40000	3
Stock..............Note B.	410	33.5	8.6	7	40000	1
Coal .... Note C.	1067, 1292					
"	1342,1345,1347					
"	1378,1414,1416					
"	1432, 1457					
"	1470, 1540	33&35	8	....	40000	22
"	1581, 1583					
....	1601,1684,1711					
"	1743,1746,1755					
....	1756 to 1761					
Hay, Special.......Note D.	1207,1221,1265	....	....	....	....	3
"	20000 to 20999	....	....	....	....	20
Total.....................						3661
Red Line..................	8800 to 8899	....	....	....	....	96
Blue Line, F. & P. M......	3500 to 3699	....	....	....	....	86
" "	3900 to 3999	....	....	....	....	37
Narrow Gauge..............	....	....	....	....	....	106
Caboose...................	....	....	....	....	....	49
Maintenance of Way........	....	....	....	....	....	37
Coal and Wood, Special....	....	....	....	....	....	24
Total						3996
Passenger.................	....	....	....	....	....	109

D., G. R. & W. AND D., L. & N. CARS.

Kind of Cars.	Numbers.	Inside Dimensions. Length	Width	Height	Capacity.	No.
Box, even Nos ....‡*	2 to 756	27.3 to 40	....	....	24 to 60000	378
" " ....∥	2000 to 2498	38	8.4	7.9	60000	250
Furniture, even Nos........	758 to 956	40	8.9	8.7½	60000	100
Stock, "	1002 to 1028	32.6	....	....	28 to 40000	14
" " ....§	1102 to 1154	§§	....	....	30 to 60000	27
Coal, odd Nos...............	1 to 7	34	8.6	8	35 & 50000	4
" Hopper bottom. ...	1093,1095,1097	20.8½	6.8	6	30000	3
" odd Nos..............	1099 to 1267	31.6	8.7	8	50000	85
" "	10001 to 10199	35	8.6	8	60000	100
Flat, " ....†	9 to 1067	28 to 37	....	....	24 to 60000	527
" "	2001 to 2399	37	8.6	8.5	60000	200
G. R. L. & D., Furniture...	1 to 100	37.6	8.4	7.8	40000	95
Total..................						1783
D. L. & N. CARS IN LINE SERVICE.						
Box, Blue Line............	5800 to 5999	38.6	7.5	6.3	30 & 40000	85
" "	6000 to 6099	33.9	8.1	6.5	40000	95
" "	6100 to 6199	33.9	8.1	6.5	40000	62
" Canada Southern Line	6501 to 6600	27.7	7.11	6.8	30000	100
" Great Eastern Line...	6200 to 6849	32.9	8.1	6.8½	30000	3
" Red Line............	1300 to 1399	34	....	....	50000	89
Cabin.....................	....	....	....	....	....	19
Maintenance of Way, etc..	....	....	....	....	....	18
Total..................						2199
Passenger..................	....	....	....	....	....	69

∥ Box cars Nos, 2006, 2046, 2106, 2135, 2193, 2224, 2312, 2382, 2488, 2452 are ventilated.

§§ Stock cars even Nos., 1102 to 1154 are 32 ft. 6 in. and 35 ft. ½ in. long, inside measurements.

§ Stock cars Nos. 1146 and 1154 are double deck.

* Nos. 112, 114, 122, 126, 136, 152, are charcoal boxes.

‡ Nos. 216, 376, 580, 656, 738, 748, are Furniture, length, 40 ft., width, 8 ft. 9 in., height, 8 ft. 7½ in., inside measurements.

† Flat cars Nos. 143, 158, 411, 569, 767, 805, 807, 895, 941 and 997 are racked for carrying barrels. No. 761 is equipped with iron tank for carrying mineral water from St. Louis to Saginaw.

C. & W. M. CARS.

Kind of Cars.	Numbers.	Inside Dimensions. Length	Width	Height	Capacity.	No.
Box, even Nos...........*¶	2 to 670	‡‡	....	....	28 to 50000	316
" " ....*‡¶	682 to 1984	‡‡	....	....	28 to 50000	592
" "	1998	33	8	6.6	40000	1
" "	2088 to 2184	33	8	6.6	40000	47
" " ....¶	2226 to 2330	33	8	6.6	40000	51
" " ....*	2338 to 2506	33	8	6.6	30 & 40000	82
" "	12000 to 12598	38	8.4	7.9	60000	300
" "	12600 to 12648	38	7.10	6.4¾	60000	18
Buggy "	2332 to 2336	45	9.8	8.10⅛	50000	3
Furniture, even Nos........	1986 to 1996	38	8.8½	8.7½	50000	6
" "	2000 to 2086	38	8.8½	8.7½	50000	44
" "	10000 to 10308	40	8.9	8.7½	60000	187
Refrigerator..............	40000 to 40198	....	....	....	....	100
Stock, even Nos., comb'n ..	672 to 680	32.4	7.10	6.10	28 & 30000	5
" " ....∥	2186 to 2224	38	8.8½	7.9	60000	20
Coal, odd Nos..............	10001 to 10039	36	8.1	8	60000	20
Flat "	1 to 2029	28 to 37	....	....	24 to 60000	488
" "	2031 to 2429	36	8.6	....	60000	195
" "	4001 to 4199	37	8.6¼	3.5	60000	100
" "	5001 to 5199	36	8.6	3.5	60000	100

PERE MARQUETTE RAILROAD--CONTINUED.

C. & W. M. CARS—Continued.

KIND OF CARS.	NUMBERS.	INSIDE DIMENSIONS.			CAPACITY	No.
		Length	Width	Height		
Flat, Pere Marquette......	16000 to 16049	36	8.6	3.5	50000	50
Silas Kilbourn & Co	100 to 103	44.3	8.9	9.7	40000	4
Stickley Bros................	1 to 9	50	8.6	9	40000	9
Wells-Higman Co	10, 15, 20	50	8.9	9	50000	3
Elk Rapids Car Co., Flats odd Nos............	1 to 199					100
Ballon Basket Co........	50	50	9	8.1		1
" "	60	59	7.10	8.3		1
Total.....						2841
IN LINE SERVICE.						
Box, Great Eastern Line ...	6350 to 6449	28.6	7.9	6.2	30000	100
" Blue Line.............	7100 to 7149	33.10	8.1	6.4	40000	48
" "	7200 to 7389	29	7.11¾	6.3¾	30000	40
Caboose...........						31
Maintenance of way, etc.....						28
Total .						3088
Passenger ...						73

*Nos. 54, 300, 304, 806, 310, 316, 346, 348. 386, 388, 390, 400, 416, 418, 420, 422, 664, 806, 962, 1006, 1040, 1070, 1072, 1306, 1358 and 2426 to 2506. even Nos. are charcoal boxes.

†Stock Cars Nos. 2190, 2192, 2194, 2200 and 2202 are double deck.

‡No. 696 is equipped for carrying chemical engines from Muskegon Chemical Engine Company.

‡‡27 ft. 6 in. to 37 ft. 4 in. long.

¶Furniture Cars Nos. 8, 10, 18, 30, 36, 50, 60, 98, 110, 114, 162, 186, 194, 198, 200, 202, 210, 230, 236, 244, 252, 268, 278, 314, 392, 398, 404, 444, 470, 500, 510, 514, 516, 524, 530, 532, 536, 542, 544, 562, 570, 590, 606, 616, 618, 650, 660, 900, 964, 1024, 1096, 1100, 1106, 1124, 1138, 1166, 1182, 2228, 14, 26, 82, 84, 40, 44, 74, 80, 96, 100, 102, 106, 112, 116, 122, 138, 146, 152, 154, 156, 182, 186, 196, 208, 216, 246, 264, 284, 294, 296, 462, 506, 518, 522, 538, 552, 568, 574, 578, 582, 584, 592, 596, 598, 606, 930, 964 are 37 ft. 4 in. long, 8 ft. 4 in. wide, 7 ft. 11 in. high. inside measurement; length 38 ft. 2 in., width at eaves 9 ft. 10 in., height to eaves 12 ft. 6 in., height to running board 13 ft. 2 in., height to top of brake staff 14 ft. 8 in., outside measurement, capacity 50000 lbs.

Box Cars 344, 424, 1436, 1586, 1588, 1596, 1598, 1602, 1606, 1610, 1612, 1614, 1618, 1622, 1624, 1626, 1628, 1630, 1684, 1636, 1640, 1642, 1644, 1646, 1652, 1654, 1656, 1660, 1662, 1670, 1678, 1680, 1682, 1684, 1686, 1688, 1692, 1694, 1696, 1700, 1702, 1704, 1706, 1710, 1712, 1714, 1716, 1718, 1722, 1728, 1780, 1732, 1738, 1740, 1744, 1746, 1748, 1750, 1764, 1756, 1762, 1766, 1768, 1770, 1776, 1778, 1782, 1784, 1786, 1788, 1790, 1792, 1794, 1796, 1798, 1802, 1804, 1806, 1810, 1812, 1814, 1816, 1818, 1820, 1822, 1824, 1826, 1880, 1834, 1836, 1838, 1840, 1842, 1848, 1850, 1852, 1854, 1856, 1858, 1860, 1862, 1866, 1868, 1872, 1874, 1884, 1886, 1888, 1890, 1892, 1894, 1898, 1900, 1902, 1906, 1908, 1910, 1914, 1918, 1920, 1922, 1924, 1926, 1930, 1932, 1936, 1940, 1942, 1944, 1946, 1948, 1950, 1952, 1954, 1960, 1964, 1966, 1968, 1970, 1972, 1974, 1976, 1978 and 1980 have been re-built ventilated. All are equipped with air brakes.

S., T. & H. CARS.

KIND OF CARS.	NUMBERS.	OUTSIDE DIMENSIONS.			CAPACITY	No.
		Length	Width	Height		
Flat	1 to 115	36	8.9	3.7	50000	115
....	151	30	7.9	5.10	40000	1
Coal	201 to 250	34	8.5	6	50000	50
....	301	34	8.10	8	50000	1
Box	501 to 525	34	8.10	8.5	50000	25
....	551, 552	30	7.2	7	40000	2
....	553 to 560	33.6	8.10	8	50000	8
Total						302

REPORTS OF MOVEMENTS.

Report movements of Great Eastern Line cars to W. H. Rosevear, Car Accountant, Grand Trunk Railway, Montreal, Quebec; Red Line cars to F. L. Pomeroy, General Manager Red Line, Buffalo, N. Y.; all other cars to David Crombie, Superintendent Transportation, Detroit, Mich.

MILEAGE REPORTS.

Send reports for mileage earned by Pere Marquette System cars as follows:

Report mileage of C. & W. M. and D. L. & N. Great Eastern Line cars to W. H. Rosevear, Car Accountant Grand Trunk Railway, Montreal, Que.

Report mileage of F. & P. M. Red Line cars to F. L. Pomeroy, General Manager Red Line, Buffalo, N. Y.

Report mileage of all other cars (making separate items as below) to H. C. Potter, Jr., Comptroller, Detroit, Mich.:

P. M.—4 - 6399.
F. & P. M.— 1-9100. except 3500-3999 & 2680-2999.
8.—S., T. & H.—1-563.
C. & W. M.—1-4199, 10001-12648.
D., G. R. & W.— 1-2498.
D. L. & N. — 10000-10199.
2—C & W. M.—5001-5199.
3—G. R., L. & D.—1-100.
D. L. & N. (Blue Line)—5800-5999.
P. M. Common—20000-20999.
4 { F. & P. M. and Blue Line— 3500- 3999, 12600-12899, 13000-13499.

5—D., L. & N. (Blue Line)—6000-6099.
6—C. & W. M.—7100-7149.
7 { C. & W. M. (Blue Line)—7200-7399.
D., L. & N., C. S. L.—6501-6600.
8 { C. & W. M. (Blue Line)—6100-6199.
D., L. & N. (Red Line)—1300-1399.
9—S. Kilbourn & Co.—100-103.
10—Stickley Bros Co.—1-9.
11—Wells-Higman Co.—10, 15 and 20.
12—Elk Rapids Car Co.—1-100.
13—Ballou Basket Co.—50 and 60.
P. M. Refrigerators—1-379.
14 { F. & P. M. Refrigerators—2680-2689.
C. & W. M. Refrigerators—40000-40199.

REPAIR BILLS.

Make o bill for repairs to all Pere Marquette (except 20,000 series), F. & P. M., C. & W. M., , G. R. & W. and S. T. & H. common cars; and send to H. C. Potter, Jr., Comptroller, Detroit, Mich.

Make separate bills for F. & P. M. Blue Line, C. & W. M. and D., G. R. & W., Canada Southern Line and Red Line, Grand Rapids, Lansing & Detroit, S. Kilbourn & Co., Stickley Bros. Co., Wells-Higman Co., Ballou Basket Co. and each series of C. & W. M. and D. G. R. & W. Blue Line and Great Eastern Line cars, and send to H. C. Potter, Jr., Comptroller, Detroit, Mich.

Make separate bills for F. & P. M. Red Line cars, and send to Peninsular Equipment Company, Detroit, Mich.

Make separate bills for Pere Marquette cars 20000 to 21999, and send to H. C. Potter, Jr., Comptroller, Detroit, Mich.

BALANCES.

For balances, remit to or draw on H. C. Potter, Jr., Comptroller, Detroit, Mich.

FREIGHT CONNECTIONS AND JUNCTION POINTS.

Ann Arbor—Alexis, O.; Alma, Mich.; Clare, Mich.; Howell Junction, Mich.; Thompsonville, Mich.; Toledo, O.

Arcadia & Betsy River—Henry, Mich.

Baltimore & Ohio—Wellsboro, Ind.

Canadian Pacific—Detroit, Mich.

Chicago & Eastern Illinois—La Crosse, Ind.

Chicago & Northwestern—Manitowoc, Wis.

Chicago, Indianapolis & Louisville — La Crosse, Ind.

Chicago, Kalamazoo & Saginaw—Woodbury, Mich.

Chicago, Milwaukee & St. Paul—Milwaukee, Wis.

Cincinnati, Hamilton & Dayton - Toledo, O.

Cincinnati Northern—Allegan, Mich.; Toledo, O.

Cleveland, Cincinnati, Chicago & St. Louis—Benton Harbor, Mich.

Detroit & Lima Northern—Carleton, Mich.; Detroit, Mich.

Detroit & Mackinac—Bay City, Mich.

Grand Rapids & Indiana—Big Rapids, Mich.; Fruitport Junction, Mich.; Grand Rapids, Mich.; Howard City, Mich.; Muskegon, Mich.; Petoskey, Mich.; Reed City, Mich.; Traverse City, Mich.

Grand Trunk—Detroit, Mich.; Ferrysburg, Mich.; Flint, Mich.; Grand Haven, Mich.; Grand Rapids, Mich.; Greenville, Mich.; Holly, Mich.; Ionia, Mich.; Muskegon, Mich.; Pt. Huron, Mich.; Saginaw, Mich.; South Lyon, Mich.; Sparta, Mich.; Trowbridge, Mich.; Wixom, Mich.; Wellsboro, Mich.

Hocking Valley—Toledo, O.

Lake Erie & Western—Belfast, Ind.

Lake Shore & Michigan Southern—Alexis, O.; Toledo, O.; Allegan, Mich.; Delray, Mich.; Detroit, Mich.; Monroe, Mich.; North Lansing, Mich.; Warner, Mich.; LaPorte, Ind.

Manistee & Grand Rapids—Canfield, Mich.; Stronach, Mich.

Manistee & North Eastern—Interlochen, Mich.; Kaleva, Mich.; Manistee, Mich.; Traverse City, Mich.

Manistee & Luther—(Narrow Gauge), East Lake, Mich.

Mason & Oceana—Ludington, Mich.

Michigan Central—Alexis, O.; Toledo, O.; Bay City, Mich.; Delray, Mich.; Detroit, Mich.; Grand Junction, Mich.; Grand Rapids, Mich.; Midland, Mich.; New Buffalo, Mich.; North Lansing, Mich.;

Paines, Mich.; Saginaw, Mich.; Vassar, Mich.; Warner, Mich.; Wayne, Mich.

New York, Chicago & St. Louis—Thomaston, Ind.

Ohio Central—Toledo, O.

Penna. Co.—Hanna, Ind., La Crosse, Ind.; Toledo, O.

Pontiac, Oxford & Northern—Clifford, Mich.

Port Huron Southern—Port Huron, Mich.

St. Joseph, South Bend & Southern—St. Joseph, Mich.

South Haven & Eastern—Hartford, Mich.

Toledo, St. Louis & Kansas City—Toledo, O.

Union Terminal Association—Delray, Mich.

Wabash—Detroit, Mich.; McGee, Ind.; Romulus, Mich.; Toledo, O.

Wheeling & Lake Erie—Toledo, O.

Wisconsin Central—Manitowoc, Wis.; Milwaukee, Wis.

December, 1900.

5

(Continued from Page 3)

Similarly, many of the earliest Pere Marquette cars lack diagrams as well. The first cars for which diagrams exist are from 1903 and, with few exceptions, they exist for all cars thereafter. Except for the new lettering, there is virtually no difference between cars built before or after the merger; all follow standard construction practices of the time. Several early car series rode on rigid-frame Fox Patent trucks, but the majority used the more common arch-bar variety. Nevertheless, there are some interesting patterns emerging even at this early date; it was the practice of the railroad to dedicate certain cars to specific industries. This is seen in the 1900 roster, which actually lists cars assigned to given shippers, especially on the Chicago & West Michigan. Notice also that Pere Marquette flat car 16449 is assigned to the service of the Thayer Lumber Company, a practice that became even more prevalent as time went on.

TOP RIGHT: Coal mine at Saginaw, with a couple of Flint & Pere Marquette two-axle cars in the foreground.

RIGHT: F&PM 30-ton "coal" car No. 9100 was equipped with drop bottom doors and arch bar trucks. It was built by American Car & Foundry in Detroit, Michigan, in 1899, part of 100 cars in lot 735. These cars were apparently the last cars received before the F&PM was consolidated into the Pere Marquette. The PM continued the number series with its own gondolas in the 9101-9200 series built by AC&F in 1900 (see Page 15).

Flint & Pere Marquette Freight Cars

ABOVE: Flint & Pere Marquette wooden furniture car No. 2802, built by the Michigan Car Company in 1888. Note the lack of an automatic coupler or brake line.

BELOW: An unusual load rides on F&PM flat car No. 1115 in the winter of 1883; a four-foot-gauge Shay locomotive for the Foster, Blackman & Sons Lumber Company of Baldwin, Michigan (Lima construction number 60).

ABOVE: F&PM No. 749, a box car built by the Michigan-Peninsular Car Company in 1898. By this time, air brakes had become standard equipment.

BELOW: Logs loaded aboard F&PM 36' flat car No. 1783 around 1895. Note the "daisy" emblem toward the near end of the car; this was the first corporate logo of the F&PM.

7

Chicago & West Michigan Railroad Freight Cars

ABOVE and ABOVE RIGHT: These two box cars were built for the Chicago & West Michigan Railroad by the Peninsular Car Works in Detroit, but the similarities end there. The furniture car is substantially taller, and the fruit car has a small sliding door in the end for ventilation purposes.

RIGHT: By 1890, when C&WM box car No. 1984 was built by the Peninsular Car Works, the Chicago & West Michigan Rail*road* had become C&WM Rail*way*, and cars were being equipped with air brakes and automatic couplers.

ABOVE: The Peninsular Car Works built C&WM 33' flat car No. 981 in 1880.
RIGHT: C&WM flat car No. 6063 was built by the Michigan-Peninsular Car Company in 1897. It carries lettering for the Thayer Lumber Company. Note the unusual hand brake consisting of two grips instead of a wheel.

Saginaw, Tuscola & Huron Railroad Freight Cars

ABOVE and LEFT: Flat cars made up more than half of the freight car fleet of the Saginaw, Tuscola & Huron Railroad before it was merged into the Pere Marquette. These two 30-ton cars, built five years apart by the Michigan-Peninsular Car Company, are remarkably similar in design.

Detroit, Grand Rapids & Western Railroad Freight Cars

AC&F Photo - MLM Collection

AC&F Photo - MLM Collection

AC&F Photo - Art Lamport Collection

ABOVE LEFT: This car was built for the Detroit, Lansing & Northern Railroad (a predecessor of the Detroit, Grand Rapids & Western) by the Michigan Car Company in Detroit, probably in the early 1880s. Note the lack of automatic coupler. The stencil in the lower left corner reads, "Car Checkers Must Report This As A Furniture Car."

ABOVE RIGHT: The Detroit, Grand Rapids & Western Railway was organized in 1896. Box car No. 2498 was built by the Michigan-Peninsular Car Company in 1898, but the *Equipment Register* places it in the same series as DL&N No. 2006 built at least 15 years prior. Note the air-brake line, automatic couplers, and the unusual Fox Patent trucks on this car.

LEFT and BELOW: DGR&W furniture car No. 956 and flat car No. 1056, were both built by the American Car & Foundry Company in Detroit, in consecutive lots (719 and 720, respectively), presumably in 1899 (the date cast into one of the flat car's wheels). AC&F was the successor to the Michigan-Peninsular Car Company, which was created when the Michigan Car Company and the Penninsular Car Works merged in 1892.

AC&F Photo - Art Lamport Collection

Pere Marquette
Railroad Freight Cars

Pere Marquette 38-foot stock car No. 2251 was built in 1908 by AC&F, series 2250-2308 (see Page 12). While previous PM stock car orders were delivered with arch bar trucks, these 30-ton cars had trucks with cast steel side frames (note the distictive H-section bottom chord). The car end has animal passage doors for two levels, and a mechanism for raising and lowering the second deck.

2000 - 2199 (1st)
2250 - 2308

Cars in series 2000-2199 were the first stock cars ordered by the Pere Marquette. Built by American Car & Foundry in 1903, these cars were of typical all-wood construction reinforced with steel truss rods. Included on the same diagram, cars 2250-2308 were built by AC&F in 1908, both series with double-deck capability. The "gap" in the number sequence is filled by cars 2200-2249 (see Page 13).

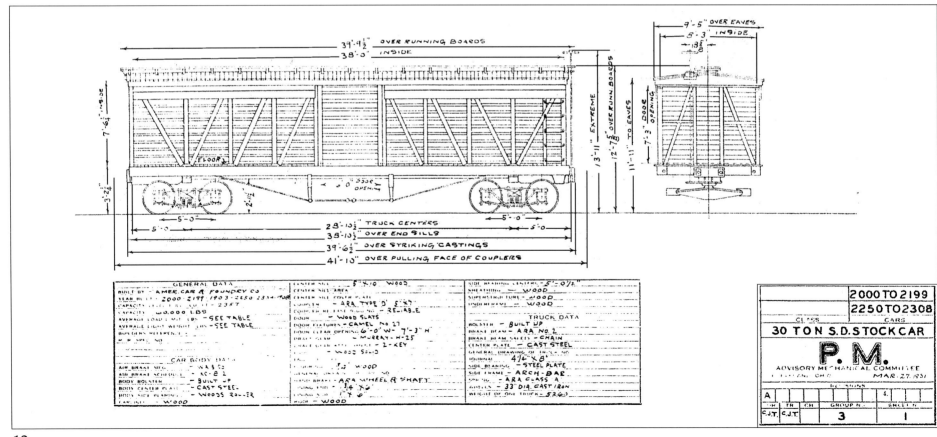

12

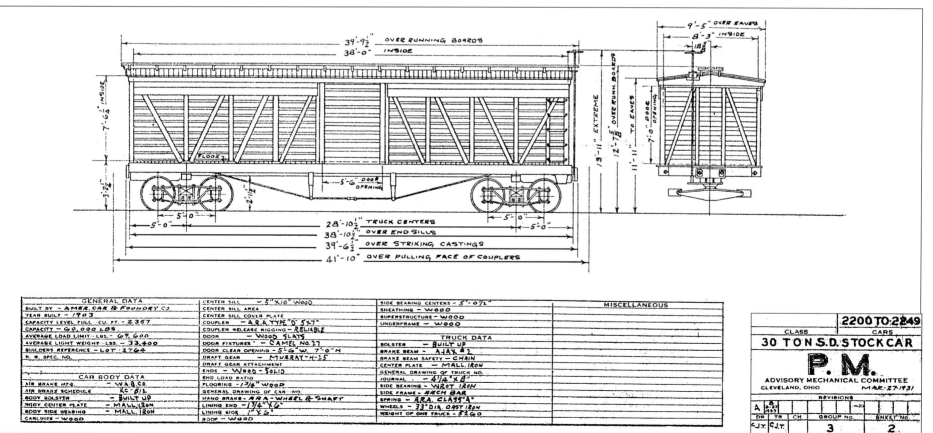

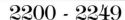
This series of fifty double-deck cars was constructed by AC&F at the same time as the 2000-2199 series in 1903. By 1929, all of these early stock cars were listed as single-deck cars within combined number series 2000-2308. All were gone by 1934.

GENERAL DATA				
BUILT BY - AMER. CAR & FOUNDRY CO	CENTER SILL - 5"X10" WOOD	SIDE BEARING CENTERS - 5'-0½"	MISCELLANEOUS	
YEAR BUILT - 1903	CENTER SILL AREA	SHEATHING - WOOD		
CAPACITY LEVEL FULL - CU. FT. - 2357	CENTER SILL COVER PLATE	SUPERSTRUCTURE - WOOD		
CAPACITY - 60,000 LBS	COUPLER - A.R.A. TYPE "D" 5"X7"	UNDERFRAME - WOOD		
AVERAGE LOAD LIMIT - LBS. - 69,600	COUPLER RELEASE RIGGING - RELIABLE			
AVERAGE LIGHT WEIGHT - LBS. - 33,400	DOOR - WOOD SLATS	TRUCK DATA		
BUILDERS REFERENCE - LOT - 2764	DOOR FIXTURES - CAMEL NO. 27	BOLSTER - BUILT UP		
R. R. SPEC. NO.	DOOR CLEAR OPENING - 5'-6" W. 7'-0" H	BRAKE BEAM - AJAX #2		
	DRAFT GEAR - MURRAY-H-25	BRAKE BEAM SAFETY - CHAIN		
	DRAFT GEAR ATTACHMENT	CENTER PLATE - MALL. IRON		
	ENDS - WOOD - SOLID	GENERAL DRAWING OF TRUCK NO.		
CAR BODY DATA	END LOAD RATIO	JOURNAL - 4¼"X8"		
AIR BRAKE MFG. - W.A.B.CO.	FLOORING - 1¾" WOOD	SIDE BEARING - WROT IRON		
AIR BRAKE SCHEDULE - KC-DIL	GENERAL DRAWING OF CAR - NO.	SIDE FRAME - ARCH BAR		
BODY BOLSTER - BUILT UP	HAND BRAKE - ARA-WHEEL & SHAFT	SPRING - A.R.A. CLASS "A"		
BODY CENTER PLATE - MALL. IRON	LINING END - 1¾"X6"	WHEELS - 33" DIA. CAST IRON		
BODY SIDE BEARING - MALL. IRON	LINING SIDE - 1"X6"	WEIGHT OF ONE TRUCK - 5260		
CARLINES - WOOD	ROOF - WOOD			

	2200 TO 2249
CLASS	CARS
30 TON S.D. STOCK CAR	

P. M.

ADVISORY MECHANICAL COMMITTEE
CLEVELAND, OHIO   MAR. 27-1931

REVISIONS						
A	2-31 1933					
DR	TR	CH	GROUP NO.		SHEET NO.	
C.J.T.	C.J.T.		3		2	

This group of 100 cars were built in 1905, also by AC&F. Although similar in appearance to the previous orders, they were only 36'0" long (inside) and were three inches wider, with a wider door opening. A note on the diagram sheet says that these cars were rebuilt in 1923, but no further information is given. Like most of their predecessors, they were off the roster by 1934. No known photo of these cars exists.

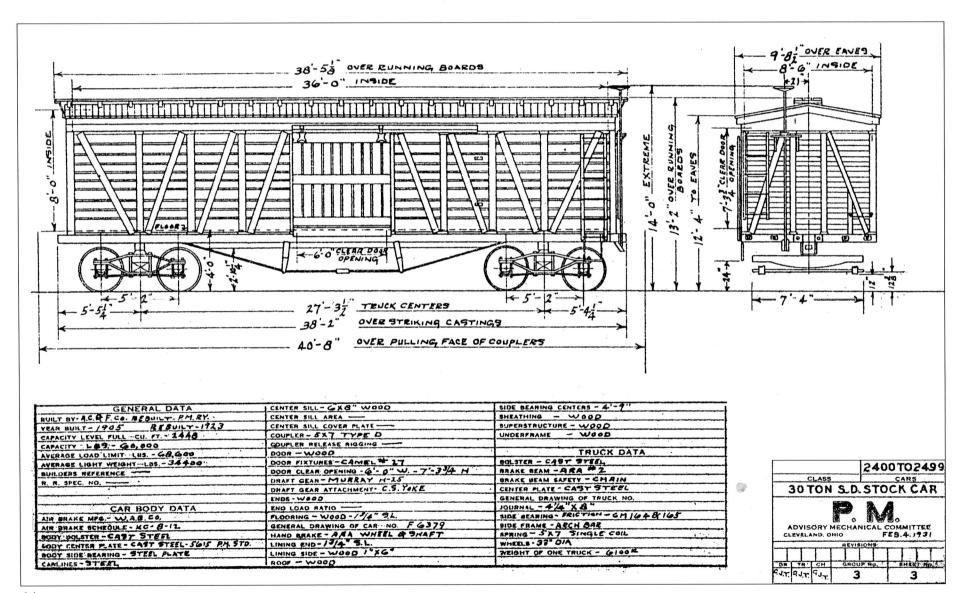

GENERAL DATA		
BUILT BY - A.C.& F. Co. REBUILT - P.M. RY.	CENTER SILL - 6"X8" WOOD	SIDE BEARING CENTERS - 4'-9"
YEAR BUILT - 1905 REBUILT - 1923	CENTER SILL AREA —	SHEATHING - WOOD
CAPACITY LEVEL FULL - CU. FT. - 2448	CENTER SILL COVER PLATE —	SUPERSTRUCTURE - WOOD
CAPACITY - LBS. - 60,000	COUPLER - 5X7 TYPE D	UNDERFRAME - WOOD
AVERAGE LOAD LIMIT - LBS. - 60,600	COUPLER RELEASE RIGGING —	
AVERAGE LIGHT WEIGHT - LBS. - 34400	DOOR - WOOD	TRUCK DATA
BUILDERS REFERENCE —	DOOR FIXTURES - CAMEL #27	BOLSTER - CAST STEEL
R. R. SPEC. NO. —	DOOR CLEAR OPENING - 6'-0" W. - 7'-3¾" H	BRAKE BEAM - ARA #2
	DRAFT GEAR - MURRAY H-15	BRAKE BEAM SAFETY - CHAIN
	DRAFT GEAR ATTACHMENT - C.S. YOKE	CENTER PLATE - CAST STEEL
	ENDS - WOOD	GENERAL DRAWING OF TRUCK NO.
CAR BODY DATA	END LOAD RATIO —	JOURNAL - 4¼" X 8"
AIR BRAKE MFG. - W.A.B. Co.	FLOORING - WOOD - 1¾" S.L.	SIDE BEARING - FRICTION - CM 164 & 165
AIR BRAKE SCHEDULE - KC-B-12	GENERAL DRAWING OF CAR - NO. F 6379	SIDE FRAME - ARCH BAR
BODY BOLSTER - CAST STEEL	HAND BRAKE - ARA WHEEL & SHAFT	SPRING - 5X7 SINGLE COIL
BODY CENTER PLATE - CAST STEEL - 5615 P.M. STD.	LINING END - 1¾" S.L.	WHEELS - 33" DIA
BODY SIDE BEARING - STEEL PLATE	LINING SIDE - WOOD 1"X6"	WEIGHT OF ONE TRUCK - 6100 #
CARLINES - STEEL	ROOF - WOOD	

	2400 TO 2499
CLASS	CARS
30 TON S.D. STOCK CAR	
P. M.	
ADVISORY MECHANICAL COMMITTEE	
CLEVELAND, OHIO	FEB. 4. 1931

REVISIONS				
DR	TR	CH	GROUP No.	SHEET No.
G.J.T.	R.J.T.	G.J.T.	3	3

Once American Car & Foundry had taken over production of the former Michigan-Peninsular Car Company plant in Detroit, it was only natural that the Pere Marquette, a long-time customer of the Michigan-based car builder, would continue the relationship. These solid bottom gondolas were built in 1899, probably the first freight cars delivered and lettered for the Pere Marquette by AC&F. Essentially flat cars with built-up sides and ends, they were constructed of wood with steel reinforcing straps and angles, supplemented by steel truss rods underneath. By this time, air brakes were standard equipment. These 30-ton cars came with Fox Patent trucks and had a 34'10" inside length. No diagram is available.

AC&F Photo - MLM Collection

9201 - 9300

Essentially the same as the 9101 series, these 30-ton cars were delivered with arch bar trucks and drop bottom doors by AC&F in 1900. By 1929, they had solid bottoms and were combined into series 9105-9400. No diagram is available.

10250 - 10999

Another series of early gondolas built by AC&F in Detroit, these 36-footers were built in 1906 and had a capacity of 40 tons. There were still 420 cars in service in 1929, but all were gone by 1934. No diagram is available.

Gordon Lydeksen Collection

This series of 40-ton gondolas was built by AC&F at the Madison, Illinois plant in 1905. They had an inside length of 36'6" and rode on arch bar trucks. The lettering for the failed *Great Central Route* makes these cars more interesting than their close cousins from Detroit. No diagram is available.

LEFT: These cars are loaded with stacked tanning bark.
BELOW: PMRR gondola No. 11229 was built in 1905 by AC&F under Lot 3479. Delivered for the combined Cincinnati, Hamilton & Dayton & Pere Marquette "System," it featured the distinctive *Great Central Route* logo.

AC&F Photo - MLM Collection

17

12000 - 12799

These cars are interesting because they have drop ends and, in that regard, differ from all other early Pere Marquette gondolas. Built by AC&F in 1903, they were retired by 1930. No diagram is available.

RIGHT: One wonders how far this load of produce, photographed in Shelby, Michigan, got before it shifted or unloaded itself.
BELOW: PM Gondola No. 12265, built in June 1903, was rated at a 40-ton capacity. Equipped with drop ends, the inside length was 35'1", almost one-and-a-half feet less than similar cars with stationary ends.

Henry Wolhout Collection

AC&F Photo - MLM Collection

18

Interstate Commerce Commission Valuation Reports - National Archives

This group of 100 cars was the most interesting of all the early Pere Marquette gondolas, because the cars featured side dump doors. AC&F built these 40-ton cars in 1903. They were only 33'4" inside and came with arch bar trucks. No diagram is available.

LEFT: PM 12800-series gondolas in ash service at Saginaw, Michigan. The structures are Robertson ash hoists.
BELOW: The 12800-series gondolas were built with five doors in each side for unloading. Notice the operating lever on the end, and the steel rod running along the side sill to lock the doors closed.

AC&F Photo - MLM Collection

19

16400 - 16899

Little is known about these flat cars. This particular 37-foot car was leased to the Thayer Lumber Company. In 1912, cars 16431, 16629, 16643, 16678, 16690, and 16829 were rebuilt to 40-ton capacity. No diagram is available.

7200 - 7207

These unknown 30-ton box cars were built before 1900 and therefore came from one of the predecessor roads. The photo shows produce being loaded into Pere Marquette double-sheathed box cars at Shelby, Michigan in 1909. No diagram is available.

Harry Wolhout Collection

20

A typical 30-ton capacity wooden box car design with truss rods, these 38-foot cars came from American Car & Foundry's Detroit, Michigan plant in 1900 as part of the Pere Marquette's first car orders. Note the Fox Patent trucks, automatic couplers, and air brakes. No diagram is available

These 38-foot box cars were built by AC&F at Detroit, in 1902. These early wooden cars were "equipped with pressed steel carlines" for greater roof support. No diagram is available.

BELOW: Pere Marquette box car No. 30196 was built in May 1902. She is a beautiful example of the PM's early lettering scheme, featuring the *Trans-Michigan Route* logo.

PMRR 36-foot wooden box car No. 32951 was built by AC&F at Madison, Illinois, in March 1905, builders lot 3478. The lettering on this car is interesting because it represents the brief (1904-1905) amalgamation of the Pere Marquette and the Cincinnati, Hamilton & Dayton to form the *Great Central Route*, which ended in the bankruptcy courts. The cars, however, operated until the great wooden-car purge of 1931, though probably with revised paint schemes. No diagram is available.

AC&F Photo - MLM Collection

40000 - 42649
43150 - 43649

This 1903 order represents one of the largest orders for cars ever placed by the Pere Marquette, over 3,000 cars. When combined with the stock cars and gondolas AC&F was building for the PM that same year, it marks 1903 as a banner year for new cars. The diagram shows that these cars were rebuilt, probably in the 1920s, with Hutchins ends, but no dates are given. Another note states that 39 cars were equipped with nine-foot staggered double doors by 1931.

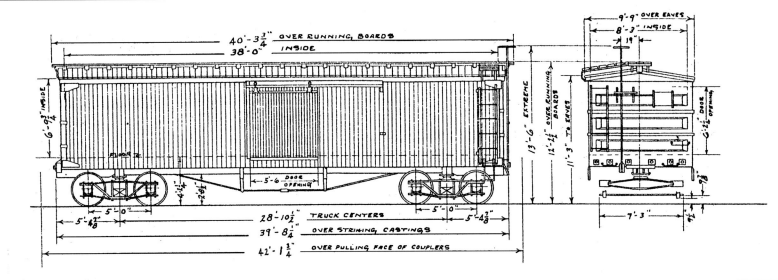

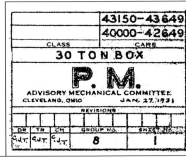

LEFT: Manistee & Northeastern Railway box car No. 41033, photographed at Manistee, Michigan, was formerly a Pere Marquette box car with the same number. M&NE received at least eleven cars from this series during the 1930s. Note the Hutchins steel end.

BELOW: Pere Marquette 30-ton box car No. 42043 was built in June 1903 by AC&F in Detroit, Michigan. This 38-foot wooden car had a capacity of 2,136 cubic feet and was equipped with automatic couplers, air brakes, and arch bar trucks. Although the diagram indicates that 71 cars from series 40000-42649 and 43150-43649 retained their original wood center sills, the others got new center sills consisting of two nine-inch, 25-pound steel channels in an undated upgrade. They also received Hutchins steel ends. There were 2,145 cars still on the roster in 1929, including 260 cars fitted with staggered nine-foot wide double doors. By 1932, only 142 cars remained in service.

RIGHT: PM No. 40073 has been repainted from its original "Trans-Michigan Route" paint scheme, displaying lettering more typical of the 1920s. This is not the distinctive Pere Marquette lettering style adopted around 1930 (note the ordinary-looking tail on the "Q" in Marquette).

OPPOSITE : Box cars were used to haul almost anything - even earth to patch up a washed-out section of roadbed, as evidenced by this 1913 photograph taken near Shelby, Michigan. This view shows the truss rods beneath PM No. 42169 to good advantage.

Interstate Commerce Commission Valuation Reports - National Archives

42650 - 43149

The cars in this series were built in 1903 in conjunction with the huge AC&F order for box cars shown on the preceding Pages (their numbers fit neatly into the series "gap"). These cars, built for transporting automobiles, were 17 inches taller inside. As with the other series, these cars were also rebuilt with Hutchins ends. The diagram states that two of these cars, No. 42930 and No. 43101, had nine-foot-wide staggered doors, and that 25 cars received full-size end doors. These were the first cars on the Pere Marquette designed to carry automobiles and were pioneers for many thousands to come.

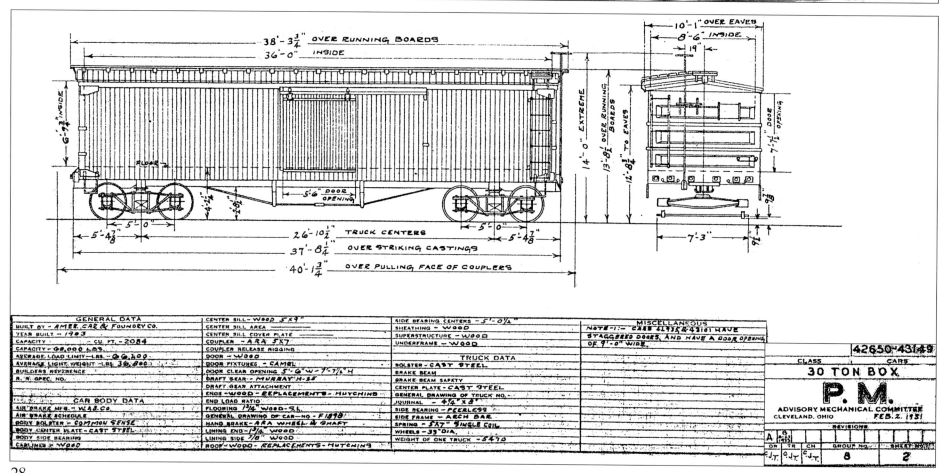

ABOVE: PM No. 42777 may still say "Vehicle" on the side in its revised paint scheme, but that's not what's inside the car. It was photographed with a C&O cousin on a siding at the Acme Limestone Company of Fort Spring, West Virginia, in about 1918. Built in 1903 by AC&F, along with 3,000-plus "standard" box cars, *Vehicle* cars in PM series 42650-43149 were only 36 feet long inside, but were wider and had an 8'3" inside height, over one-and-a-half feet taller than the box cars. Note that the diagram for these cars utilizes the same "drawing" as for the box cars shown on Page 24. Although the dimensions have been altered for the vehicle cars, the inside height remains incorrect. In 1929, almost 300 of these cars were still on the roster in general service.

50000 - 53999

This massive order for 4,000 box cars was built by The Pullman Company in 1906-1909. They were quite similar in appearance and dimensions to the 36-foot 42650-43149 series *Vehicle* cars built by AC&F in 1903, but were rated at 40 tons capacity. Cars in series 52500-52999 were built with seven-foot wide doors and assigned to automobile service. Like the previous AC&F box cars, the original wooden ends were replaced with Hutchins steel ends, and the center sills were upgraded with steel channels. Other notes indicate that various cars later received staggered double doors.

RIGHT: PM 36-foot general service box car No. 50685 was built in March 1909 under Pullman Lot 5188 with six-foot doors. The lettering scheme has been simplified slightly – the "period" after the *Pere Marquette* road name has been dropped and the car lacks the attractive *Trans-Michigan Route* logo.

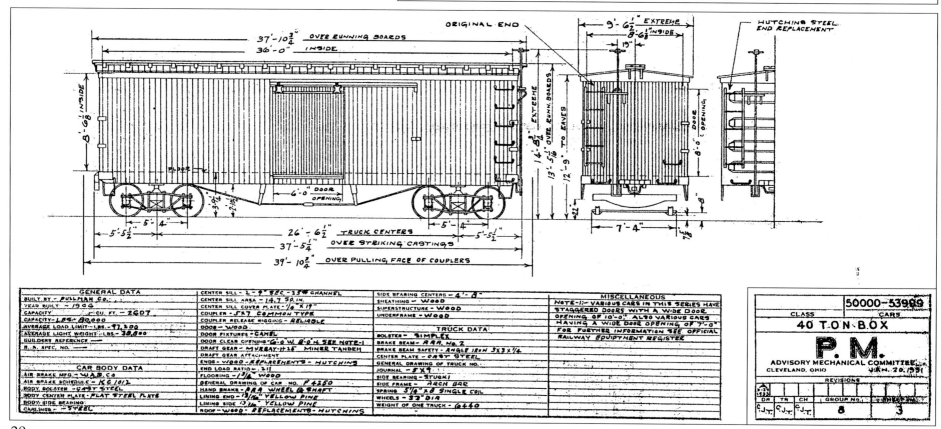

LEFT: Pere Marquette No. 50881, at Newaygo, Michigan, approximately 1910.

BELOW: Pere Marquette No. 50326 with a revised lettering scheme after a 1914 repainting.

PLM Photo - Art Lamport Collection

BOTH: These two cars have seven-foot doors, reason enough for them to carry the "Automobile" designation. In 1906 the Pere Marquette ordered 4,000 box cars from Pullman, which were constructed during 1906-1909 under three known lots: 5145, 5164, and 5188. Auto car No. 52575 (above) was built in December 1906 under lot 5145, while auto car No. 52815 (right) was delivered in March 1909 under lot 5188 (the same as box car 50685 on Page 30). Auto car No. 52987 (opposite Page), which came in 1907 under lot 5164. The diagram book gives no information about which cars were assigned to which lots, and only lists 1906 as the built date for the entire series.

PLM Photo - FCJ Collection, Courtesy of Jim Kinkaid

LEFT: Pere Marquette auto car No. 52987 was built in February 1907, one of the 500 cars in series 52500-52999 with seven-foot doors. By 1929, only 129 cars remained in the original configuration. Two hundred cars rebuilt with staggered doors were still in service, all assigned to general merchandise loading. They were retired by the mid-1930s.

LEFT: Pere Marquette No. 53575 originally had a six-foot door opening centered on the car side. The opening has been enlarged to ten feet, extending to the right of center on either side. The majority of the cars in this series were eventually equipped with staggered door openings for automobile service; some were nine-feet wide and others were ten-feet wide. By 1932, less than 600 cars from the original order were still on the roster.

34

2 The Reorganization Era

World War I brought many changes to America's railroads. For freight equipment, these changes could be summed up in one word . . . steel. The first all-steel cars in America were hopper cars built in 1896 for the Bessemer & Lake Erie Railroad. The B&LE also pioneered in all-steel box cars in 1908. It's not a coincidence that B&LE was wholly owned by Carnegie Steel Corporation. While wide acceptance of all-steel cars remained for the future, increased use of steel for components gained much wider acceptance, particularly for underframes. Gradually, this trend came to include ends, roofs, and sides on box cars. Hoppers, gondolas, and flat cars used in bulk service achieved all-steel status more quickly as the advantages of their more rugged construction were seen to offset the disadvantages of their additional weight. By the end of the 1930s, most freight cars were of all-steel construction.

During this period, the Pere Marquette established many trends that were to carry over to the very end of its existence as an independent road. It was the era of the United States Railroad Administration when, due to the wartime emergency, the United States Government took over the running of the nation's railroads. Not only did the government operate the railroads, it also designed and ordered locomotives and cars for their use. The Pere Marquette received 3,000 of these cars.

The guns had hardly fallen silent and the railroads returned to civilian control when the Pere Marquette embarked on the first of many car rebuilding programs. Indeed, the entire history of Pere Marquette freight cars becomes immensely more complex at this point because of the proliferation of these rebuildings, which continued right to the end of independent operation in 1947, and was even continued beyond that by the Chesapeake & Ohio Railway.

Another complicating factor, this one typically Pere Marquette, enters the picture now as well. Though it's common railroad practice to assign certain cars to specific industries, the Pere Marquette began to renumber cars assigned to dedicated services into series bearing little or no relation to the cars' original numbers. These renumberings are covered in more detail in the diagrams and roster notes. This can lead to some confusion, because although the diagram may make one think that (for example) cars in the 66000 series were added to those in the 89000 series, it merely means that several of the 89000 series cars have been renumbered into the 66000 series because of the industry they serve. That same basic series can end up with three or four offshoot number series, indicating that cars from that series are dedicated to three or four different industries. They are really the same cars with the numbers changed.

Pere Marquette pioneered in the use of special interior fastenings, due primarily to the highly specialized nature of its automobile industry traffic. This included the special racks built on gondolas to handle auto frames, as well as interior racks to carry finished automobiles in their box cars. The growth of automobile and auto parts traffic and the decline of agricultural products is reflected in increasing numbers of forty and fifty-foot double-door box cars, and the phasing out of stock cars. All of these changes are a direct reflection of the changing economy in the Pere Marquette's area of Michigan.

These were the final stock cars on the Pere Marquette. They were converted from auto cars 89300-89349 by the Wyoming Shops at Grand Rapids in 1934. The original cars were built by the Pressed Steel Car Company in 1927. The ten-foot door opening of the auto cars necessitated three smaller side panels to the left of the double doors. When the four-foot auxiliary door opening was filled in for the conversion, the result was the unique four-three side panel spacing of the stock cars.

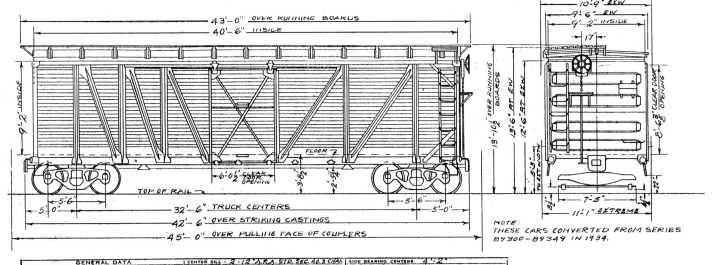

ABOVE: PM stock car No. 2000, just out of the Wyoming Shops in February 1934, is representative of the 50 stock cars rebuilt from single-sheathed auto cars numbered 89300-89349 (see Page 74). However, this particular car has a built date of October 1926, indicating that it was originally one of the Canadian-built cars from the identical 88000 series (see Page 71).

NOTE:
THESE CARS CONVERTED FROM SERIES
89300-89349 IN 1934.

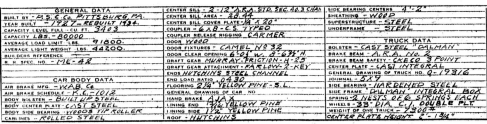

GENERAL DATA		
BUILT BY - P.S.C. Co. PITTSBURG, PA.	CENTER SILL - 2-12" A.R.A. STD. SEC. 40.3 CHAN	SIDE BEARING CENTERS - 4'-2"
YEAR BUILT - 1927 - REBUILT 1934.	CENTER SILL AREA - 28.44	SHEATHING - WOOD
CAPACITY LEVEL FULL - CU. FT. 3403	CENTER SILL COVER PLATE - ¼ X 20"	SUPERSTRUCTURE - STEEL
CAPACITY LBS.- 80000	COUPLER - 6 X 8 - C.S. TYPE D	UNDERFRAME - STEEL
AVERAGE LOAD LIMIT - LBS. 91800.	COUPLER RELEASE RIGGING - CARMER	
AVERAGE LIGHT WEIGHT - LBS. 44200.	DOOR - WOOD	TRUCK DATA
BUILDERS REFERENCE -	DOOR FIXTURES - CAMEL No. 32	BOLSTER - CAST STEEL "DALMAN"
R. R. SPEC. NO. - MC-42.	DOOR CLEAR OPENING 6'-0¼" W. 8'-6¾" H.	BRAKE BEAM - A.R.A. No. 2
	DRAFT GEAR - MURRAY-FRICTION-H-25	BRAKE BEAM SAFETY - C.K.E CO. 3 POINT
	DRAFT GEAR ATTACHMENT - FARLOW-2-KEY	CENTER PLATE - CAST INTEGRAL
	ENDS - HUTCHINS STEEL CHANNEL	GENERAL DRAWING OF TRUCK NO. Q-19316
CAR BODY DATA	END LOAD RATIO .0430	JOURNAL - 5 X 9
AIR BRAKE MFG - WAB. Co.	FLOORING 2¼" YELLOW PINE - S.L.	SIDE BEARING - HARDENED STEEL
AIR BRAKE SCHEDULE - K.C.-1012	GENERAL DRAWING OF CAR NO.	SIDE FRAME - DALMAN INTEGRAL BOX
BODY BOLSTER - BUILT UP STEEL	HAND BRAKE - AJAX	SPRING - 2 NESTS OF 6 SPRINGS EACH
BODY CENTER PLATE - CAST STEEL	LINING END - 1½" YELLOW PINE	WHEELS - 33" DIA. C.I. DOUBLE PLT.
BODY SIDE BEARING - WOODS TIP ROLLER	LINING SIDE - 1½" YELLOW PINE	WEIGHT OF ONE TRUCK - 7300 #
CARLINES - ROLLED STEEL	ROOF - HUTCHINS	CENTER PLATE HEIGHT - 2'-1¾"

	2000-2049
CLASS	CARS
40 TON S.D. STOCK CARS	

P M
ADVISORY MECHANICAL COMMITTEE
CLEVELAND, OHIO   SEPT. 11, 1934.

REVISIONS

GROUP NO.	SHEET NO.
3	1

LEFT: This end view of PM hopper No. 13512 shows the original ratchet-type hand brake applied to these cars. It was probably a *Perfection* brand and, according to the diagram, was later replaced by a *Blackall* ARA type.

The cars in the 13000 series were built for the United States Railroad Administration and assigned to the Pere Marquette. They were built to USRA specification 1005-B as fifty-ton cars. Ralston Steel Car Company built Nos. 13000-13499, while AC&F built Nos. 13500-13999. Cars 13525-13999 were originally delivered lettered and numbered GET (Government Equipment Trust) 36517-37027 and 37400-37447. They were relettered and numbered shortly before delivery. They were the first open-top hoppers on the Pere Marquette.

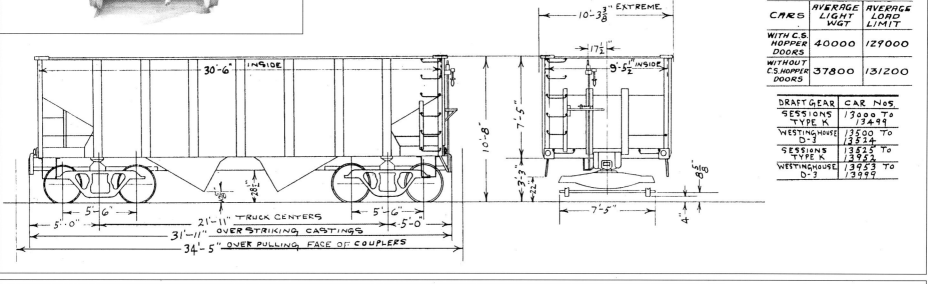

CARS	AVERAGE LIGHT WGT	AVERAGE LOAD LIMIT
WITH C.S. HOPPER DOORS	40000	129000
WITHOUT C.S. HOPPER DOORS	37800	131200

DRAFT GEAR	CAR NOS.
SESSIONS TYPE "K"	13000 TO 13499
WESTINGHOUSE D-3	13500 TO 13524
SESSIONS TYPE "K"	13525 TO 13952
WESTINGHOUSE D-3	13953 TO 13999

GENERAL DATA		
BUILT BY - 13000-13499 RALSTON, 13500-13999-AC&F	CENTER SILL - 12"-35# S.B. CHANNEL.	SIDE BEARING CENTERS - 4'-2"
YEAR BUILT - 1919-20	CENTER SILL AREA - 24.5 SQ.IN.	SHEATHING —
CAPACITY LEVEL FULL CU.FT. - 1889	CENTER SILL COVER PLATE-12½" X 5/16"	SUPERSTRUCTURE- STEEL
CAPACITY WITH 10 IN. HEAP CU.FT.- 2120	COUPLER — ARA TYPE "D"	UNDERFRAME — STEEL
AVERAGE LOAD LIMIT LBS.- SEE TABLE	COUPLER RELEASE RIGGING-CARMER & IMPERIAL	
AVERAGE LIGHT WEIGHT LB:-SEE TABLE	DOOR — AJAX. SEE NOTE-1	
BUILDERS REFERENCE	DOOR FIXTURES ENTERPRISE	TRUCK DATA
R. R. SPEC. NO. M.E.29	DOOR CLEAR OPENING —	BOLSTER - CAST STEEL
	DRAFT GEAR-SEE TABLE	BRAKE BEAM - DAMASCUS #2
	DRAFT GEAR ATTACHMENT - C.S. YOKE	BRAKE BEAM SAFETY - CRECO - 3-POINT
	ENDS — 3/16" STEEL	CENTER PLATE - C.S. & CAST INTEGRAL.
CAR BODY DATA	END LOAD RATIO - .054	GENERAL DRAWING OF TRUCK NO.- Q-16494
AIR BRAKE MFG. - W.A.B.CO	FLOORING — ¼" STEEL	JOURNAL - 5½ X 10
AIR BRAKE SCHEDULE - K D-1012	GENERAL DRAWING OF CAR NO. 139-10-184	SIDE BEARING - STUCKI
BODY BOLSTER - PRESSED STEEL	HAND BRAKE - BLACKALL, REPLMENT- ARA	SIDE FRAME-ANDREWS C.S.
BODY CENTER PLATE - C S	LINING END —	SPRING - B 5-15- DOUBLE COIL
BODY SIDE BEARING - STEEL PLATE	LINING SIDE —	WHEELS - 33" CAST IRON DOUBLE PLATE
CARLINES —	ROOF —	WEIGHT OF ONE TRUCK — 8600"
		CENTER PLATE HEIGHT- 2'-1¾"

MISCELLANEOUS
NOTE-1 - CAST STEEL HOPPER DOORS BEING APPLIED. 796 CARS COMPLETED. AS OF 11-29-37

U.S.R.A.

13000-13999

CLASS   CARS
50 TON HOPPER

P. M.
ADVISORY MECHANICAL COMMITTEE
CLEVELAND, OHIO   DEC - 13-1936.

REVISIONS

GROUP NO.   SHEET NO.
4   1

ABOVE: Pere Marquette two-bay hopper No. 13512 was built by AC&F at its Berwick, Pennsylvania, plant in March 1920. These 55-ton hoppers were equipped with Andrews trucks. They were the first all-steel freight cars on the PM, lasting into the early 1950s on the C&O. The diagram sheet states that the Ajax hopper doors were being replaced by cast steel doors, with 796 cars completed as of November 11, 1937.

RIGHT: PM 13808 in service at Waverly (Holland), Michigan, in 1940. It's painted in the most modern PM lettering scheme.

The 500 cars in this series were virtual duplicates of the 13000 series, differing primarily in their use of Bettendorf T-section trucks instead of Andrews. Though built to the USRA plans, they were constructed by Ralston Steel Car of Columbus, Ohio, some three years after the demise of the USRA.

LEFT: PM No. 14458 is shown at Grand Rapids on December 15, 1935, still equipped with the ratchet hand brake.

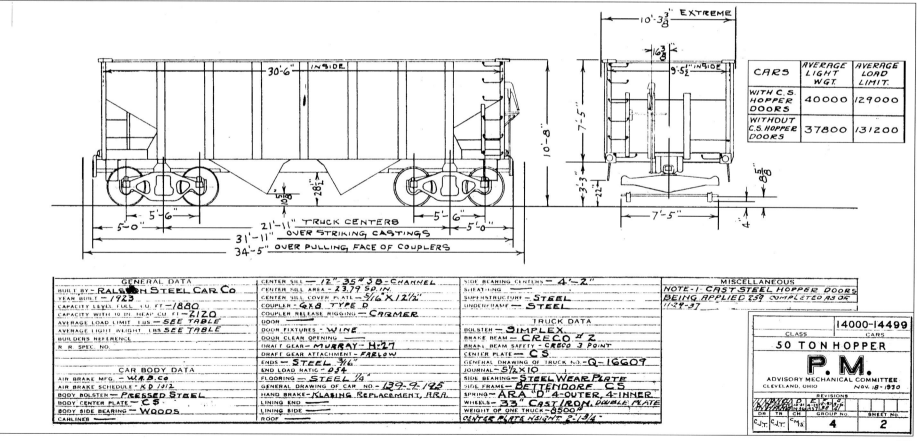

CARS	AVERAGE LIGHT WGT.	AVERAGE LOAD LIMIT.
WITH C.S. HOPPER DOORS	40000	129000
WITHOUT C.S. HOPPER DOORS	37800	131200

GENERAL DATA

BUILT BY -	RALSTON STEEL CAR Co.
YEAR BUILT -	1923
CAPACITY LEVEL FULL CU. FT. -	1880
CAPACITY WITH 10 IN. HEAP CU. FT. -	2120
AVERAGE LOAD LIMIT. LBS -	SEE TABLE
AVERAGE LIGHT WEIGHT LBS	SEE TABLE
BUILDERS REFERENCE	
R. R. SPEC. NO.	

CAR BODY DATA

AIR BRAKE MFG. -	W.A.B.Co.
AIR BRAKE SCHEDULE -	KD 1012
BODY BOLSTER -	PRESSED STEEL
BODY CENTER PLATE -	CS
BODY SIDE BEARING -	WOODS
CARLINES -	

CENTER SILL -	12" 35# SB - CHANNEL
CENTER SILL AREA -	23.79 SQ. IN.
CENTER SILL COVER PLATE -	5/16" X 12 1/2"
COUPLER -	6X8 TYPE D
COUPLER RELEASE RIGGING -	CARMER
DOOR	
DOOR FIXTURES -	WINE
DOOR CLEAR OPENING	
DRAFT GEAR -	MURRAY - H-27
DRAFT GEAR ATTACHMENT -	FARLOW
ENDS -	STEEL 3/16"
END LOAD RATIO -	.054
FLOORING -	STEEL 1/4"
GENERAL DRAWING OF CAR NO. -	139-9-195
HAND BRAKE -	KLASING REPLACEMENT, ARA
LINING END -	
LINING SIDE -	
ROOF	

SIDE BEARING CENTERS -	4'-2"
SHEATHING	
SUPERSTRUCTURE -	STEEL
UNDERFRAME -	STEEL

TRUCK DATA

BOLSTER -	SIMPLEX
BRAKE BEAM -	CRECO #2
BRAKE BEAM SAFETY -	CRECO 3 POINT
CENTER PLATE -	CS
GENERAL DRAWING OF TRUCK NO. -	Q-16609
JOURNAL -	5 1/2 X 10
SIDE BEARING -	STEEL WEAR PLATE
SIDE FRAME -	BETTENDORF CS
SPRING -	ARA "D" 4-OUTER, 4-INNER
WHEELS -	33" CAST IRON. DOUBLE PLATE
WEIGHT OF ONE TRUCK -	8500#
CENTER PLATE HEIGHT -	2-13/4"

MISCELLANEOUS

NOTE-1: CAST STEEL HOPPER DOORS BEING APPLIED 259 COMPLETED AS OF 11-29-37

14000-14499	
CLASS	CARS
50 TON HOPPER	

P.M.

ADVISORY MECHANICAL COMMITTEE.
CLEVELAND, OHIO · NOV. 18-1930

REVISIONS			
DR	TR	CH	GROUP NO.	SHEET NO.
C.J.T.	C.J.T.	C.M.S.	4	2

ABOVE: "The Ralston Steel Car Company, of Columbus, Ohio, is making delivery of the 500 steel hoppers, which were recently ordered. These cost, in all, about $845,000. They bear the series numbers of 14000 to 14499, inclusive." - *Pere Marquette Service Magazine, June 1923.* PM two-bay hopper No. 14109, built to the USRA design, was delivered in April 1923. A number of railroads, including the Pere Marquette, continued to order USRA-type freight cars, sometimes with slight variations, well into the 1920s. Note the Bettendorf T-section trucks and the continued use of ratchet hand brakes, which were being replaced with Klasing ARA type in the 1930s.

The 250 cars in this series were built by Standard Steel Car Company in 1927. They were the only 70-ton hoppers on the Pere Marquette, and were the last open top hoppers of any type purchased by the road. The PM's entire hopper car fleet of 1,750 cars was constructed in a brief seven-year span. These triple hoppers were equipped with Ajax power hand brakes, Ajax hopper doors, Enterprise Type "D" door operating mechanisms, KD 10-12 brake systems, and Dalman 70-ton trucks. They lasted well into the C&O era. In 1954, there were still 142 cars on the roster, but all were gone within a couple of years.

ABOVE: With a few exceptions, these PM cars follow the late 1920s Enterprise Railway Equipment Company design for 70-ton offset-side 10-post triple hoppers. Drawings can be found in the 1928 and 1931 *Car Builders' Cyclopedias*. The Enterprise hopper was an alternative to the American Railroad Association (ARA) 1926 design for a 70-ton offset-side 11-post quadruple hopper (Class 4E-HT). Although both designs had "compound-stepped" end side sheets, the PM cars utilized a "sloped-stepped" version along with the Enterprise *Side Construction* and hopper layout. They also received the distinctive ARA pressed steel end side sills that showed up on the revised ARA 70-ton quad hopper design (4E-HT-2) adopted in 1929. With other refinements, the Enterprise triple hopper design ultimately evolved into the familiar Association of American Railroads (AAR) 1935 Standard 70-ton offset-side hopper with "sloped end side sheets."

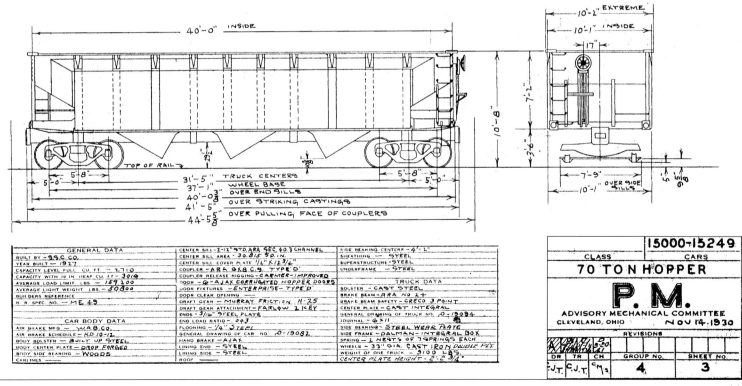

16000 - 16099 (2nd)

Built in 1930 by Bethlehem Steel Company at Johnstown, Pennsylvania, these were the only 42-foot steel flat cars on the Pere Marquette. Although not built by the United States Railroad Administration (USRA), this series of flat cars was constructed to the USRA *design* created a decade prior to their delivery.

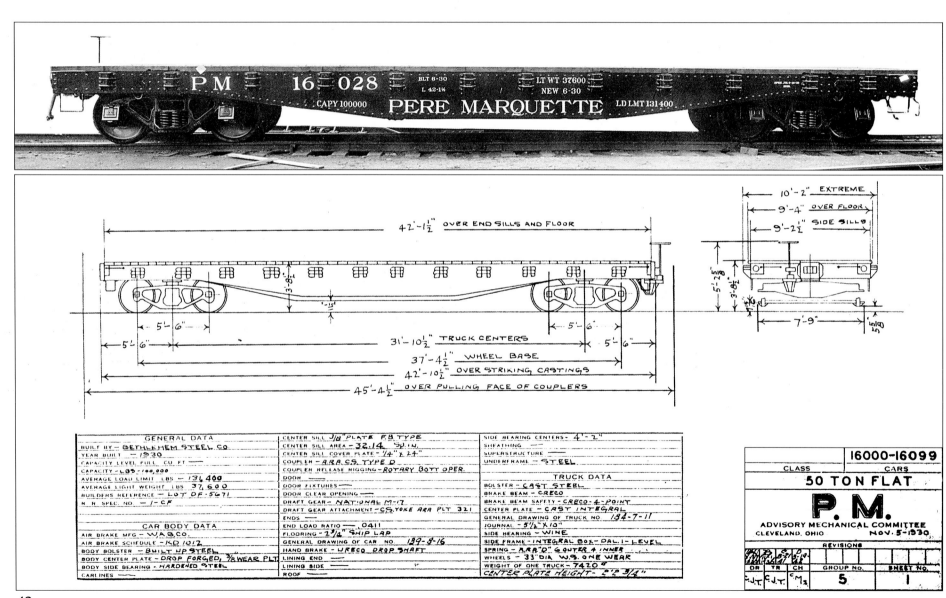

ABOVE and OPPOSITE: Pere Marquette 50-ton flat car No. 16028 was delivered in June 1930 as part of an order for 100 steel cars built to the USRA plans. Except for the uneven spacing of the cast-steel stake pockets (the USRA design had "even" spacing) and slightly wider floor boards, these PM cars otherwise match the dimensions of the USRA drawings. Even though the USRA didn't build flat cars of this type, the design was popular and was utilized by over a dozen railroads in the 1920s. The PM cars had KD 10-12 brake equipment, a Ureco drop-shaft hand brake, and Dalman trucks. At the time of the C&O merger, there were still 98 cars in service. Almost half of these remained in 1954, but within two years the ranks were reduced to ten.

	16500
CLASS	CARS

40 TON FLAT

P.M.

ADVISORY MECHANICAL COMMITTEE
CLEVELAND, OHIO   MAY. 27, 1931.

REVISIONS

A	B	C 11-1 1935					
DR	TR	CH	GROUP NO.		SHEET NO.	
C.J.T.	C.J.T.		5		2	

In 1930, Pere Marquette converted this unusual car for service by the Magnetic Springs Water Company of Saginaw, Michigan. Rather than use a flat car, they took USRA box car No. 81279 and cut it down, creating the bed on which the tank, thought to have been furnished by the water company, rested. There are no known photos of this car, which was dismantled when service ended in 1941.

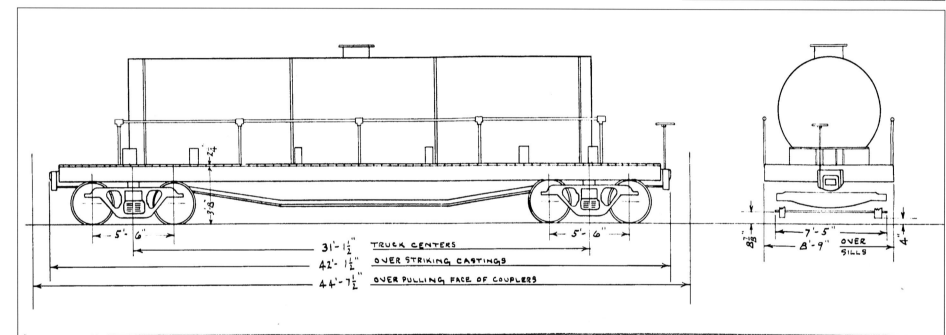

31'-1½" TRUCK CENTERS
42'-1½" OVER STRIKING CASTINGS
44'-7½" OVER PULLING FACE OF COUPLERS
5'-6"   5'-6"
7'-5" 8'-9" OVER SILLS

GENERAL DATA				MISCELLANEOUS
BUILT BY - SEE NOTE	CENTER SILL - BUILT UP - F.B. TYPE	SIDE BEARING CENTERS - 4'-1"		NOTE THIS CAR WAS CONVERTED FROM
YEAR BUILT SEE NOTE	CENTER SILL AREA - 28.64 SQ.IN.	SHEATHING		40 TON BOX CAR NO. 81279 - ORIGINALLY
CAPACITY LEVEL FULL CU.FT	CENTER SILL COVER PLATE - 20½ X ¼"	SUPERSTRUCTURE		WAS BUILT BY THE McGUIRE CAR CO. IN 1919
CAPACITY WITH 10 IN. HEAP CU.FT	COUPLER - ARA TYPE "D"	UNDERFRAME - STEEL		-1920 - AND REBUILT BY THE P.M. RY. IN 1930.
AVERAGE LOAD LIMIT LBS - 93,500	COUPLER RELEASE RIGGING - CARMER	TRUCK DATA		THIS CAR IS USED BETWEEN ST. LOUIS, MICH. &
AVERAGE LIGHT WEIGHT LBS - 42,500	DOOR	BOLSTER - CAST STEEL - U.S.S. PATT.		SAGINAW, MICH. AND IS EQUIPPED TO CARRY
BUILDERS REFERENCE	DOOR FIXTURES	BRAKE BEAM - CRECO NO. 2+		WATER TANK OWNED BY MAGNETIC SPRINGS
R.R. SPEC. NO.	DOOR CLEAR OPENING	BRAKE BEAM SAFETY - CRECO - 3 POINT		WATER CO. OF SAGINAW, MICH.
	DRAFT GEAR - SESSIONS	CENTER PLATE - C.S		
	DRAFT GEAR ATTACHMENT- C.S. YOKE	GENERAL DRAWING OF TRUCK NO.- 9-1645B		
CAR BODY DATA	ENDS	JOURNAL - 5X9		
AIR BRAKE MFG. - W.A.B.Co	END LOAD RATIO - 035	SIDE BEARING		
AIR BRAKE SCHEDULE - KC-1012	FLOORING	SIDE FRAME - CAST STEEL		
BODY BOLSTER - PRESSED STEEL	GENERAL DRAWING OF CAR NO.	SPRING - ARA - CLASS "C"		
BODY CENTER PLATE - DROP FORGED	HAND BRAKE - ARA WHEEL	WHEELS - 33" DIA. C.I. DOUBLE PLATE		
BODY SIDE BEARING - HARDENED STEEL	LINING END	WEIGHT OF ONE TRUCK - 6720#		
CARLINES	LINING SIDE			
	ROOF			

Pere Marquette Service Magazine

ABOVE: Built in 1927, PM gondola No. 17090 had eight drop-bottom doors and drop ends.

These 55-ton composite gondolas were built in 1927 by the Illinois Car & Manufacturing Company at Hammond, Indiana. They featured Hutchins drop ends and eight Enterprise drop-bottom doors. The original wood side sheathing was replaced with steel between 1932 and 1940 (the diagram shows the steel side version). The drop-bottom doors were replaced with solid floors beginning in 1944, with the last cars remaining in service until 1954.

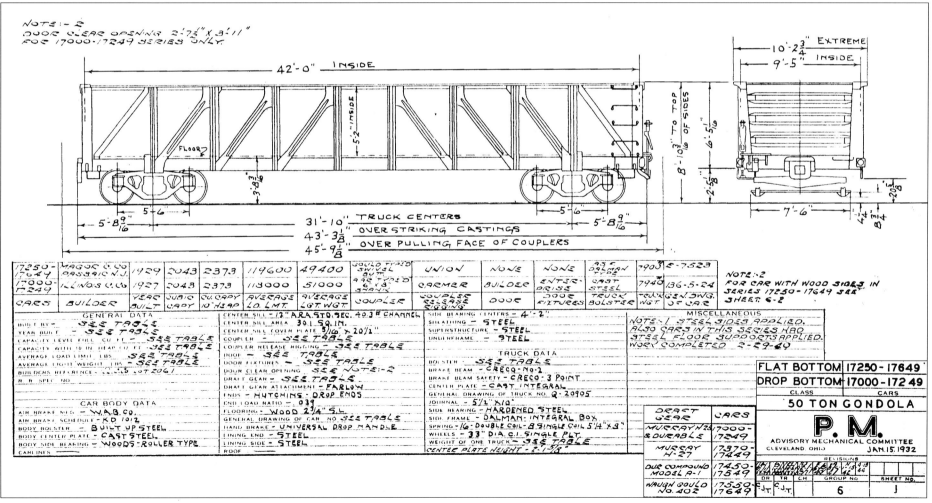

17250 - 17649

The 400 cars in this series were built as composite side gondolas by Magor Car Corporation at Passaic, New Jersey, in 1929. Like the earlier 17000-series cars, they also had Hutchins drop ends, but differed in having solid floors. The diagram shows the car as-built with wooden sides, which were replaced with steel sheathing by 1942.

ABOVE: PM gondola No. 17354, at Wellsboro, Indiana, on November 1, 1952, was rebuilt with steel sides.

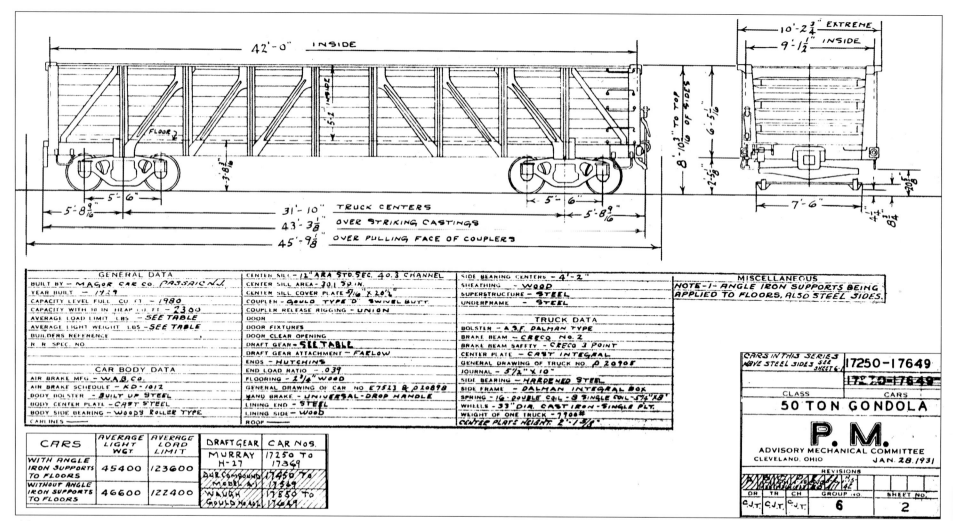

GENERAL DATA		
BUILT BY — MAGOR CAR CO. PASSAIC N.J.		
YEAR BUILT — 1929		
CAPACITY LEVEL FULL CU FT — 1980		
CAPACITY WITH 10 IN. HEAP CU FT — 2300		
AVERAGE LOAD LIMIT LBS — SEE TABLE		
AVERAGE LIGHT WEIGHT LBS — SEE TABLE		
BUILDERS REFERENCE		
R.R. SPEC. NO.		

CAR BODY DATA		
AIR BRAKE MFG — W.A.B. CO.		
AIR BRAKE SCHEDULE — KD-1012		
BODY BOLSTER — BUILT UP STEEL		
BODY CENTER PLATE — CAST STEEL		
BODY SIDE BEARING — WOODS ROLLER TYPE		
CARLINES —		

CENTER SILL — 12" ARA STD. SEC. 40.3 CHANNEL		
CENTER SILL AREA — 30.1 SQ IN.		
CENTER SILL COVER PLATE — 9/16" X 20½"		
COUPLER — GOULD TYPE "D" SWIVEL BUTT		
COUPLER RELEASE RIGGING — UNION		
DOOR		
DOOR FIXTURES		
DOOR CLEAR OPENING		
DRAFT GEAR — SEE TABLE		
DRAFT GEAR ATTACHMENT — FARLOW		
ENDS — HUTCHINS		
END LOAD RATIO — .039		
FLOORING — 2¼" WOOD		
GENERAL DRAWING OF CAR NO. E7523 & P20898		
HAND BRAKE — UNIVERSAL-DROP HANDLE		
LINING END — STEEL		
LINING SIDE — WOOD		
ROOF —		

SIDE BEARING CENTERS — 4'-2"		
SHEATHING — WOOD		
SUPERSTRUCTURE — STEEL		
UNDERFRAME — STEEL		

TRUCK DATA		
BOLSTER — A.S.F. DALMAN TYPE		
BRAKE BEAM — CRECO NO. 2		
BRAKE BEAM SAFETY — CRECO 3 POINT		
CENTER PLATE — CAST INTEGRAL		
GENERAL DRAWING OF TRUCK NO. P 20905		
JOURNAL — 5½" X 10"		
SIDE BEARING — HARDENED STEEL		
SIDE FRAME — DALMAN INTEGRAL BOX		
SPRING — 16 DOUBLE COIL - 8 SINGLE COIL - 5¼" X 8"		
WHEELS — 33" DIA. CAST IRON - SINGLE PLT.		
WEIGHT OF ONE TRUCK — 7900#		
CENTER PLATE HEIGHT — 2'-1⅝"		

MISCELLANEOUS		
NOTE-1 — ANGLE IRON SUPPORTS BEING APPLIED TO FLOORS. ALSO STEEL SIDES.		

CARS	AVERAGE LIGHT WGT	AVERAGE LOAD LIMIT	DRAFT GEAR	CAR NOS.
WITH ANGLE IRON SUPPORTS TO FLOORS	45400	123600	MURRAY H-27	17250 TO 17369
WITHOUT ANGLE IRON SUPPORTS TO FLOORS	46600	122400	DUR COMPOUND MODEL A	17450 TO 17569
			WAUGH	17850 TO
			GOULD MODEL	17649

CARS IN THIS SERIES HAVE STEEL SIDES SEE SHEET 6

17250-17649

~~17250-17649~~

CLASS

50 TON GONDOLA

P.M.
ADVISORY MECHANICAL COMMITTEE
CLEVELAND, OHIO   JAN. 28, 1931

REVISIONS

DR	TR	CH	GROUP NO	SHEET NO.
C.J.T.	C.J.T.	C.J.T.	6	2

ABOVE: The details of Pere Marquette composite gondola No. 17250 can be seen clearly in this builder's photograph taken in June 1929. Although the PM's 17000 and 17250-series gondolas are very similar to the USRA design, they actually follow the Enterprise Railway Equipment company arrangement shown in the 1928 *Car Builders' Cyclopedia*. The Enterprise/PM gondola was seven-inches higher (six-inches inside) than the USRA car, and had 6'6" tall side posts, compared to the USRA's 5'8" and 5'11" posts. The most noticeable difference is the redesigned side sill, which provided better clearance for the eight drop-bottom doors. While the floor boards on the USRA car sat directly on top of the nine-inch side sill channel and were visible from the outside, the Enterprise version had the boards resting on the short leg of a full-length 5"x3-1/2"x3/8" angle, much like the side sill design of the 1932 ARA box car. The lower edge of the side sill was strengthened with a full-length 4"x3-1/2"x1/2" bulb angle. The resulting nine-inch high, double-angle side sill combination was located higher on the car side with the underframe components more visible than on the USRA design. The new side sill arrangement required a redesigned bolster connection with a large mounting plate. Note the

stirrup step mounting plate and the location of the poling pocket on the end sill. The PM cars differed from the Enterprise design slightly in that they were six-inches longer inside and were equipped with Hutchins drop ends, which necessitated the use of 12-inch channel end sills located below the floor line and connected to the draft gear box. To maintain clearance when the ends were removed, a Universal drop-shaft hand brake was mounted on the corner post. Only the first 250 of the PM's composite gondolas had drop-bottom doors. The 400 cars in series 17250-17649 had solid bottoms, but were otherwise identical. Both series had split-K (KD) brake systems. In 1937, 388 of the solid bottom cars were equipped with racks for auto frame loading. The remaining 12 cars had their wood sides replaced with steel. By 1940, 201 cars were still in auto frame service, with the remaining 199 cars listed as having steel sides and a capacity of 2043 cubic feet. By 1942, the auto frame cars were gone and all had steel sides. The 17000-17249 series cars also received new steel sides and eventually, solid bottoms. At that point, the two series were virtually the same. In 1950, there were still 466 of the original 650 cars on the roster but by 1954, only three remained.

The Enterprise Side Sill

These 750 40-foot gondolas were the last of their kind on the Pere Marquette, as all subsequent orders were for 50-foot cars. Products of Ralston Steel Car Company in 1929, they were also the only series of 40-foot gondolas built new with steel sides. During the mid-1930s, 175 of these cars were modified by the addition of end racks for transporting automobile frames. Beginning in 1946, modified cars were renumbered into two separate sub-series, 10000-10099 and 10200-10299. The cars were renumbered at random, and no record exists to identify which 17000 series cars were used. A shop drawing for the rack doesn't exist, and it may have been homemade by the shops.

RENUMBERINGS

PM SERIES	FIRST APPEARED	DESCRIPTION
10000-10049	1946	Plymouth Auto Frames
10050-10099	1946	Cadillac and Packard Auto Frames
10200-10299	1946	Plymouth Auto Frames

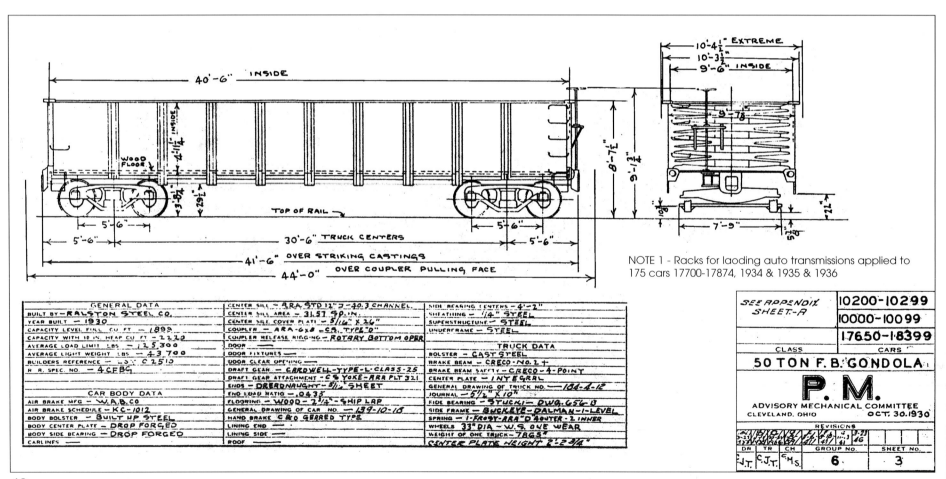

NOTE 1 - Racks for laoding auto transmissions applied to 175 cars 17700-17874, 1934 & 1935 & 1936

PM
1 765 0
CAPY 100000
LD LMT 126000
LT WT 43000 NEW 5-30

PE RE
MA RQ UE TT E

IL 40-6
I W 9-6
BLT 5-30 CU FT 2221

PM17650

RET VA 86138

IW WS WHLS

No 2 + B B

PM17650

PM
17650 -18349

ABOVE: PM gondola No. 17840, photographed in Flint, Michigan on November 12, 1935, had been modified with an auto frame rack at Grand Rapids the preceding February. A total of 175 gondolas, numbers 17700-17874, received these racks between 1934 and 1936. The racks were removed when automobile production was curtailed during World War II; but by 1946, 73 cars in series 10000-10099 and 50 cars in series 10200-10299, had been renumbered and re-equipped for handling auto frames.

RIGHT and PRECEDING PAGE: The Pere Marquette bolstered their gondola fleet in 1930 with the addition of 750 all-steel 40-foot gondolas in series 17650-18349 built by Ralston Steel Car Company. These 50-ton cars had wood floors, Dreadnaught steel ends, KC 10-12 brake equipment, geared staff hand brakes, and Dalman 1-level trucks.

ABOVE: Pere Marquette gondola No. 17782 was photographed at Plymouth, Michigan, on November 26, 1933. It's being held by the claims department, possibly due to being involved in a lawsuit against the railroad (note the word "hold" chalked near the end of the car). This general service car was reweighed four months prior at Ottawa Yard, in Erie, Michigan. PM's 40-foot all-steel gondolas are probably better known for their use in shipping automobile frames, with 95 cars still assigned to this service as late as 1954. At the same time, 142 cars from the 17650 series were still listed, as well as 507 cars, which had been renumbered into C&O series 217650-218349, thus accounting for 744 of the original cars (no doubt upgraded with AB brakes). By 1957, there were only 70 cars in auto frame service, six cars in the 17650 series, and 134 cars in C&O series 217650. Most were retired within a few years, but 18 cars with C&O numbers soldiered on until 1961.

18400 - 18649

At the same time the Pere Marquette purchased its last 40-foot gondolas from Ralston Steel Car Company in 1930 (series 17650-18399), Greenville Steel Car Company was building the first of the 50-foot gondolas. The built dates are virtually identical. These 70-ton gondolas were equipped with Dreadnaught drop ends and Klasing drop-handle hand brakes. A note on the diagram sheet states that cars 18450-18534 were converted for auto frame service in 1940, and assigned to general service during most of WWII. In 1945 these 85 cars were renumbered into the 10100-10184 series, placing them between the two series of renumbered 40-foot cars (see Page 48). Also, cars 18400-18449 had their insides lined with wood two inches thick for stone service in 1939. This lining was removed by 1944, and the cars continued in service until 1974.

RENUMBERINGS

PM SERIES	FIRST APPEARED	DESCRIPTION
10100-10199	1945	Cadillac, Oldsmobile, and Packard Auto Frames

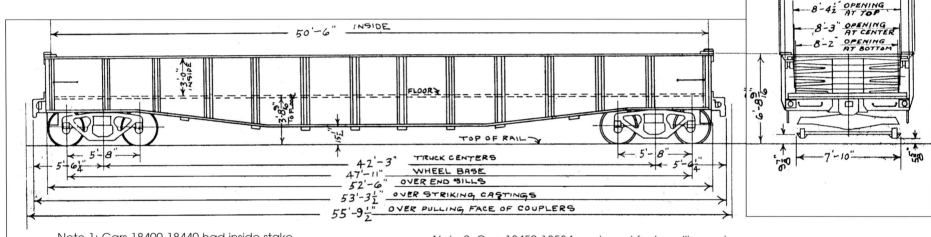

Note 1: Cars 18400-18449 had inside stake pockets removed & wood lining applied to sides on inside of car for stone trade.

Note 2: Cars 18450-18534 equipped for handling auto frames. June to Dec. 1940.

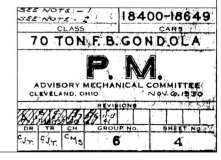

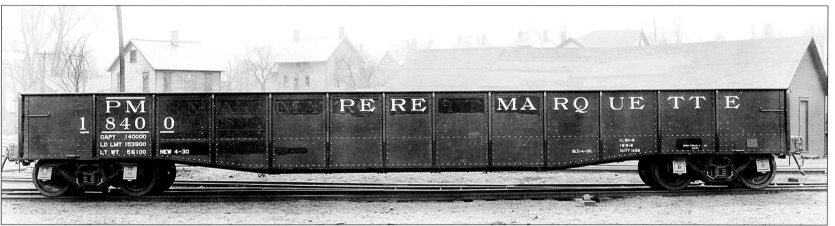

All three photographs on this page show the same car, but there are some interesting differences. The top photograph was taken first. By the time the center photograph was taken, the lettering had been changed twice (we suspect that a new requirement for the PM reporting marks to be displayed might have been the cause for the relettering). A close examination of this photograph shows that the *Pere Marquette* road name had been lettered beginning on the panel next to the reporting marks; it was probably moved further to the right to eliminate confusion. The lettering scheme shown below is the one that was finally adopted for these cars. But when this car was given a dull coat of paint for its acceptance photograph, there was still another change made: the "NEW" and "BLT" dates were changed from April to May of 1930! Plans for this series can be found in the 1937 and 1940 *Car Builders' Cyclopedias.*

ABOVE: PM gondola No. 10144 with a load of auto frames at Ludington, Michigan, in 1946. Reweighed at Wyoming Shops in Grand Rapids in October 1945, it was probably repainted and renumbered at this time. The modification for auto frame service included the metal protrusions at the bottom of the second panel in from each end (note the weight stenciling has been moved one panel to the right to accommodate this). Originally, 85 cars, numbers 18450-18534, were converted for auto frame loading in 1940. During WWII, the cars were relagated to general service due to the curtailment of automobile manufacturing by the War Production Board. As auto production began to resume in 1945, 80 of the cars were reassigned to auto frame service and were renumbered into series 10100-10199. These cars continued in this assignment well into the C&O era. In 1954, there were still 67 auto frame cars, supplemented by cars 18404 and 18455, and an additional 29 cars from the C&O's (ex-PM) 218400-218649 series. At this time, there were also 136 cars in general service including 117 cars from the 218400 series. By 1965, 23 cars were still hauling auto frames, with one car, No. 218529, listed as being equipped for handling truck cabs. Just 29 general service cars remained.

RENUMBERINGS

PM SERIES	FIRST APPEARED	DESCRIPTION
66001-66025	1938	Motor Hubs and Drums
67001-67010	1938	Kelsey-Hayes Co. Wheels
69001-69004	1940	Chemical Service

Western Michigan near the shore of Lake Michigan has long been known for the variety and abundance of fruit and vegetables grown there. In 1924, the Pere Marquette constructed 300 refrigerator cars in the Wyoming Shops especially for this trade. They had an interesting history. In 1939, 131 cars were retired and sold to Hyman-Michaels Co. In 1940, 125 cars were sold to Fruit Growers Express and were renumbered into their 16100-16299 series. Thirty-nine of the remaining cars were converted to insulated box cars comprising three different number series: 66001-66025, 67001-67010, and 69001-69004 (see table).

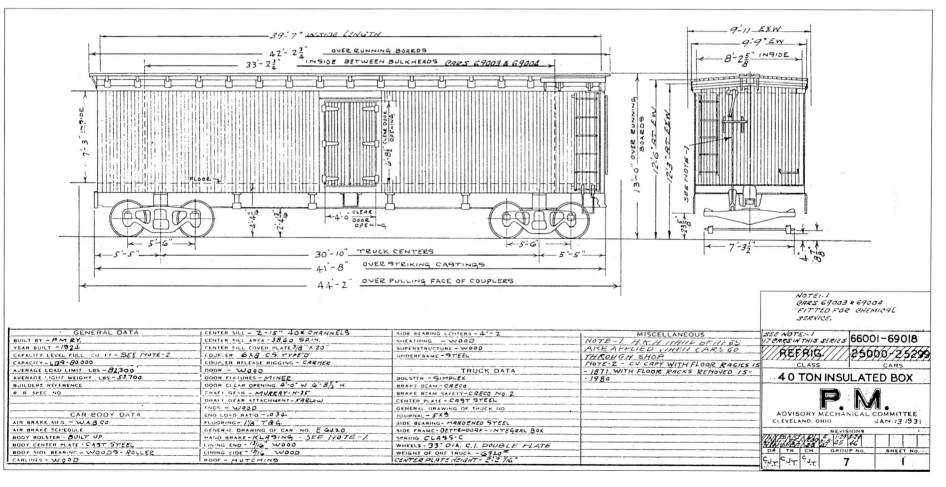

ABOVE: In 1924, the Pere Marquette's company forces completed sample refrigerator car No. 25000, the prototype for the first of 300 such cars built at the Wyoming Shops. Perhaps the most interesting thing about these cars is they were built new by the PM from Fruit Growers Express company plans and were not rebuilds of older cars.

National Archives of Canada - Merrilees Collection - PA 187334

ABOVE: This in-service view of PM reefer No. 25101 nicely shows the roof, hatches, roof platforms, and the end details typical of the original cars. Note the Klasing ratchet hand brake, then popular with the PM. These wood roofs were replaced with Hutchins steel roofs by 1930.

ABOVE: This former PM reefer became FGEX No. 16134 and survives at the Puget Sound & Snoqualmie Valley Railroad at Snoqualmie, Washington.

The Haskell & Barker Car Company originally built these 1,000 cars in 1917-1918 with ten-foot door openings and wooden ends as shown in the diagram. Most, if not all, had their wooden ends replaced with Hutchins steel ends. Many cars also had single, six-foot doors applied. About half of these cars were retired between 1934 and 1936. By that time, all remaining cars had six-foot door openings.

ABOVE: This rare photograph of a PM 70000-series box car (No. 70874) with a ten-foot door opening is enlarged from a 1929 yard scene in Pittsburgh, Pennsylvania.

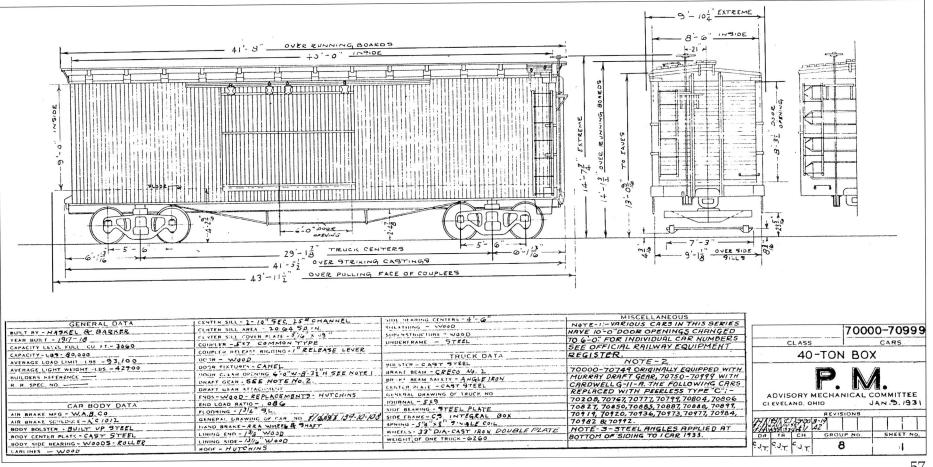

ABOVE: PM wood side box car No. 70416, at Manitowoc, Wisconsin, on September 21, 1933. Around 1930, it was converted to a single door car with a six-foot door opening. Note the Hutchins steel replacement end on this car. The diagram sheet indicates that these cars had steel underframes, but the presence of truss rods suggests that the underframes were probably wood rebuilt with steel center sills, bolsters, and cross-members. Although rather late in the development of freight cars, it was not unusual for railroads to order wooden box cars with truss rods in the mid-to-late 'teens.

ABOVE: Pere Marquette USRA box car No. 81808 was built by Pacific Car & Foundry in 1920. It has been nearly impossible to locate quality photographs of the PM's USRA box cars.

RENUMBERINGS

PM SERIES	FIRST APPEARED	DESCRIPTION
61001-61404	1937	Buick Motors and Gas Tanks
61041-61050	1942	Buick Motors and Gas Tanks
62001-62015	1937	Buick Axles
64001-64050	1938	
67050-67054	1941	Kelsey Hayes Castings
69045-69054	1941	Chevrolet Castings
69055-69099*	1941	Chevrolet Castings

*from series 80000-80499 (12-foot door openings)

USRA box cars converted to box-express cars by PM in 1920

X-513 from 80438	Standard Steel Car Company
X-514 from 80792	Standard Steel Car Company
X-515 from 80087	Standard Steel Car Company
X-516 from 80524	Standard Steel Car Company
X-517 from 80426	Standard Steel Car Company
X-518 from 80407	Standard Steel Car Company
X-519 from 80205	Standard Steel Car Company
X-520 from 81767	Pacific Car & Foundry Company
X-521 from 80203	Standard Steel Car Company
X-522 from 80924	Standard Steel Car Company
X-523 from 80744	Standard Steel Car Company
X-524 from 80565	Standard Steel Car Company
X-525 from 80347	Standard Steel Car Company
X-526 from 80802	Standard Steel Car Company
X-527 from 80629	Standard Steel Car Company
X-528 from 80845	Standard Steel Car Company
X-529 from 80934	Standard Steel Car Company
X-530 from 80321	Standard Steel Car Company
X-531 from 80013	Standard Steel Car Company
X-532 from 80853	Standard Steel Car Company

X-800 to X-818 converted by PM in 1923 from 80000-80499 series cars (Individual car numbers were not listed).

The 2000 double-sheathed box cars in this series were assigned to the Pere Marquette by the United States Railroad Administration in 1920. They came from four different builders as follows:

80000-80999   Standard Steel Car Company
81000-81109   Keith Car & Manufacturing Company
81110-81323   McGuire Car Company
81324-81999   Pacific Car & Foundry Company

Originally, the USRA had allocated 500 single-sheathed box cars to the Pere Marquette, but when the final allocations were made, they were assigned 2,000 of the double-sheathed type. These box cars were all built to USRA specifications, number 1003-B; the PM received no single-sheathed cars. In 1920, twenty of the USRA box cars were taken at random and converted to box-express cars X513-X532. Again in 1923, PM took nineteen more cars and converted them into box-express cars X800-X818. Between 1925 and 1927, at least 478 cars in series 80000-80499 were rebuilt with 12-foot door openings and double Camel wood doors (see Page 61). The remaining cars received internal modifications and fittings for specific services, and many were renumbered as they were assigned to specific industries. As a test, six cars had their original Murphy roof replaced with Hutchins steel roofs in 1933. By the following year, all of the double-door rebuilds in series 80000-80499, plus 139 of the single-door cars, had Hutchins roofs applied. There is one final chapter to the story of the PM USRA box cars. In 1937, the Minneapolis & St. Louis railroad acquired 150 ex-PM cars via the Hyman-Michaels Company and renumbered them into their 25000-25298 (even) series. In addition, the Duluth, South Shore & Atlantic railroad purchased 100 ex-PM cars in 1939 from Haffner-Thrall, placing them in series 16000-16099.

RIGHT: Pere Marquette Maintenance-of-Way box car No. TS-6 is a former 80000-series USRA box car photographed at Saginaw, Michigan, in June 1959. The USRA box cars served the PM well, with the last of the original six-foot door cars remaining in revenue service until the end of WWII. Several continued to serve the Pere Marquette District of the Chesapeake & Ohio as MofW cars, as in this example. A number of railroads rebuilt their USRA box cars to all-steel cars, usually of higher capacity, however, the PM decided to invest in new AAR design steel box cars instead.

RIGHT: One of twenty box cars converted by the PM to box-express service shortly after they were built, PM X-517 was photographed at Muskegon on May 11, 1938. Thirteen cars within Nos. X-513 to X-531 were still in revenue service in 1949, according to the *Official Register of Passenger Train Equipment*. Despite the changes to the side doors, ends, and trucks, this is one of the better illustrations of some of the construction features of the USRA box cars.

LEFT: PM USRA box car No. 80162 was rebuilt to a double-door car with a 12'0" door opening for automobile service in the mid-1920s. By 1926, 250 cars had been completed and, shortly thereafter, the remaining cars from series 80000-80499 were also converted, thus requiring a separate listing in the *Equipment Register*. By 1940, fewer than 200 of the double-door cars remained, with 45 being assigned to auto parts service. In 1941, these XAP cars were renumbered into series 69055-69099, with the last few being retired in 1946.

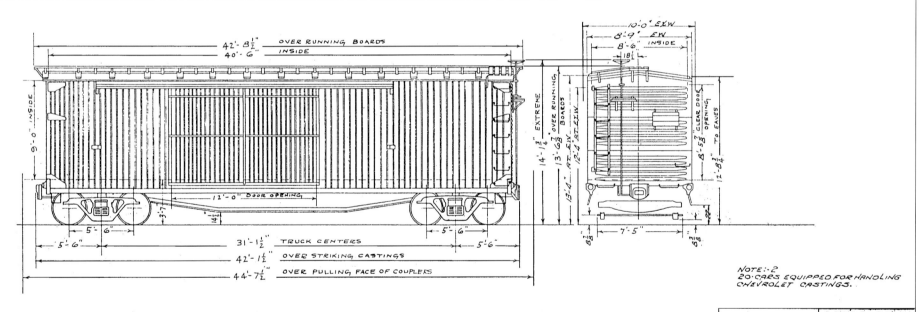

NOTE:-2
20 CARS EQUIPPED FOR HANDLING
CHEVROLET CASTINGS.

GENERAL DATA			MISCELLANEOUS
BUILT BY - STANDARD STEEL CAR CO.	CENTER SILL - BUILT UP STEEL	SIDE BEARING CENTERS - 4'-2"	
YEAR BUILT - 1920	CENTER SILL AREA - 20.645 SQ. IN.	SHEATHING - 13/16"	NOTE - 1 - CARS IN THIS SERIES EQUIPPED WITH S. H. STEEL ROOFS
CAPACITY LEVEL FULL CU. FT. - 3098	CENTER SILL COVER PLATE 1/4" X 20 1/2"	SUPERSTRUCTURE - WOOD	
CAPACITY WITH 10 IN. HEAP CU. FT. -	COUPLER - ARA 6X8 TYPE D	UNDERFRAME - STEEL	
AVERAGE LOAD LIMIT LBS - 91,600	COUPLER RELEASE RIGGING - CARMER		
AVERAGE LIGHT WEIGHT LBS - 44,400	DOOR - CAMEL	TRUCK DATA	
BUILDERS REFERENCE -	DOOR FIXTURES - CAMEL CO.	BOLSTER - PRESSED STEEL & CAST STEEL	
R. R. SPEC. NO. -	DOOR CLEAR OPENING - 12'-0" W 8-5/8" H	BRAKE BEAM - CRECO NO. 2	
	DRAFT GEAR - WESTINGHOUSE D-3	BRAKE BEAM SAFETY - CRECO 3 POINT	
CAR BODY DATA	DRAFT GEAR ATTACHMENT - CAST STEEL YOKE	CENTER PLATE - CAST STEEL	
AIR BRAKE MFG. - W.A.B. CO.	ENDS - MURPHY STEEL	GENERAL DRAWING OF TRUCK NO -	
AIR BRAKE SCHEDULE - KC 1012	END LOAD RATIO - .035	JOURNAL - 5X9	
BODY BOLSTER - PRESSED STEEL	FLOORING - 2 1/4" T&G	SIDE BEARING - ROLLER TYPE - WINE, STUCKI & WOODS	
BODY CENTER PLATE - DROP FORGED	GENERAL DRAWING OF CAR- NO - 199-11-159	SIDE FRAME - ANDREWS C.S.	
BODY SIDE BEARING - HARDENED STEEL	HAND BRAKE - ARA WHEEL & SHAFT	SPRING - ARA CLASS "C"	
CARLINES - PRESSED STEEL	LINING END - 13/16" WOOD T&G	WHEELS - 33" DIA. C.I. DOUBLE PLATE	
	LINING SIDE - 13/16" WOOD	WEIGHT OF ONE TRUCK - 6720#	
	ROOF - MURPHY-XLA TYPE - REPLACED WITH HUTCHIN	TRUCK CENTER PLATE HEIGHT - 2'-1 3/4"	

SEE NOTE:-2 | **80000-80499**
CLASS | CARS
40 TON AUTO BOX
P. M.
ADVISORY MECHANICAL COMMITTEE
CLEVELAND, OHIO — APRIL. 23. 1931
REVISIONS
DR | TR | CH | GR'P | NO. | SHEET NO.
C.J.T. | C.J.T. | C.J.T. | | 8 | 20

80500 - 81999

RIGHT: Strawbridge & Clothier in Philadelphia appears to be receiving a train-load of merchandise in Pere Marquette USRA box cars (date unknown).

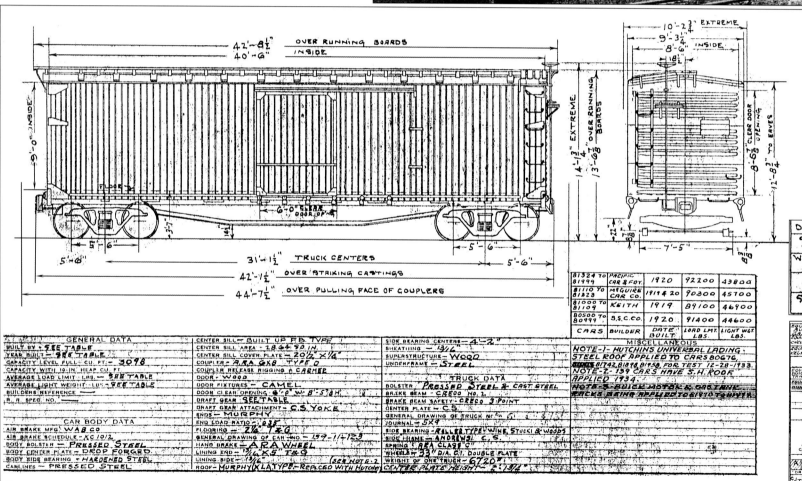

DRAFT GEAR	CAR NOS.
SESSIONS TYPE K	80500 TO 80999
WESTINGHOUSE D3	81000 TO 81109
"	81110 TO 81323
SESSIONS TYPE K	81324 TO 81999

CARS	BUILDER	DATE BUILT	LOAD LMT. LBS.	LIGHT WGT. LBS.
81324 TO 81999	PACIFIC CAR & FDY.	1920	92200	43800
81110 TO 81323	MCGUIRE CAR CO.	1919 & 20	90300	45700
81000 TO 81109	KEITH	1919	89100	46900
80500 TO 80999	S.S.C.CO.	1920	91400	44600

GENERAL DATA

BUILT BY -	SEE TABLE
YEAR BUILT -	SEE TABLE
CAPACITY LEVEL FULL - CU. FT. -	3098
CAPACITY WITH 10-IN. HEAP CU. FT.	
AVERAGE LOAD LIMIT - LBS.	SEE TABLE
AVERAGE LIGHT WEIGHT - LBS.	SEE TABLE
BUILDERS REFERENCE -	
R.R. SPEC. NO.	

CAR BODY DATA

AIR BRAKE MFG	WAB CO
AIR BRAKE SCHEDULE -	KC 10/2
BODY BOLSTER -	PRESSED STEEL
BODY CENTER PLATE -	DROP FORGED
BODY SIDE BEARING -	HARDENED STEEL
CARLINES -	PRESSED STEEL

CENTER SILL -	BUILT UP R.B. TYPE
CENTER SILL AREA -	28.64 SQ. IN.
CENTER SILL COVER PLATE -	20½" X ¼"
COUPLER -	A.R.A. 6X8 TYPE D
COUPLER RELEASE RIGGING	CARMER
DOOR -	WOOD
DOOR FIXTURES -	CAMEL
DOOR CLEAR OPENING -	6'0" W 8'5⅛H
DRAFT GEAR	SEE TABLE
DRAFT GEAR ATTACHMENT -	C.S. YOKE
ENDS -	MURPHY
END LOAD RATIO -	.035
FLOORING -	2½" T & G
GENERAL DRAWING OF CAR NO. -	199-1/4-129
HAND BRAKE -	ARA WHEEL
LINING END -	1¹⁵/₁₆" X5" T & G
LINING SIDE -	¹³/₁₆" (SEE NOTE-2)
ROOF -	MURPHY (X LA TYPE - REPLACED WITH HUTCHINS)

SIDE BEARING CENTERS -	4'-2"
SHEATHING -	¹³/₁₆"
SUPERSTRUCTURE -	WOOD
UNDERFRAME -	STEEL

TRUCK DATA

BOLSTER	PRESSED STEEL & CAST STEEL
BRAKE BEAM -	CRECO NO. 2
BRAKE BEAM SAFETY -	CRECO 3 POINT
CENTER PLATE -	C.S.
GENERAL DRAWING OF TRUCK NO.	
JOURNAL -	5X9
SIDE BEARING -	ROLLER TYPE WINE, STUCKI & WOODS
SIDE FRAME -	ANDREWS C.S.
SPRING -	ARA CLASS C
WHEELS -	33" DIA. C.I. DOUBLE PLATE
WEIGHT OF ONE TRUCK -	6720"
CENTER PLATE HEIGHT -	2'-1¾"

MISCELLANEOUS

NOTE-1- HUTCHINS UNIVERSAL LADING. STEEL ROOF APPLIED TO CARS 80976.
CARS 81742,81896,81950 FOR TEST 12-28-1933.
NOTE-2- 159 CARS HAVE S.H. ROOF APPLIED 1934.
NOTE-3- BUICK MOTOR & ORLEANS RACKS BEING APPLIED TO 8110 TO 81199

EQUIPPED FOR HANDLING BUICK MOTORS (OR) 1931 TRUCKS	81041-81050
EQUIPPED FOR HANDLING CHEVROLET CASTINGS	69045-69099
EQUIPPED FOR HANDLING KELSEY HAYES CASTINGS	67050-67057
	64001-64050
EQUIPPED FOR HANDLING BUICK MOTORS (OR) 1931 TRUCKS 5-1-1937	61001-61040
EQUIPPED FOR HANDLING BUICK AXLES 5-19-1937	62001-62085

U.S.R.A.	80500-81989
CLASS	CARS

40 TON BOX

P.M.

ADVISORY MECHANICAL COMMITTEE
CLEVELAND, OHIO DEC 13, 1934

REVISIONS

GROUP NO. 8   SHEET NO. 2

In 1922, the Pere Marquette ordered 1,000 of these double-door auto cars from Western Steel Car & Foundry, and an additional 1,500 nearly identical cars from Pressed Steel Car Company to better handle the increasing shipping needs of the automobile industry. Within a few years, the PM further expanded their fleet by modifiying almost 500 USRA single-door box cars into similar double-door cars with 12-foot door openings. However, after purchasing nearly 3,000 larger capacity 40' and 50' all-steel auto cars in the 1930s, these wood sided cars with ten-foot door openings became less useful. In 1937, the PM began to convert the 1922-built auto cars into single-door box cars by either rebuilding to single six-foot door cars or by permanently sealing the auxiliary doors shut. All were converted by 1943. Some cars were renumbered and assigned to specific services starting in 1945, with the last of the cars on the active roster until 1957.

1922 Car Builder's Cyclopedia

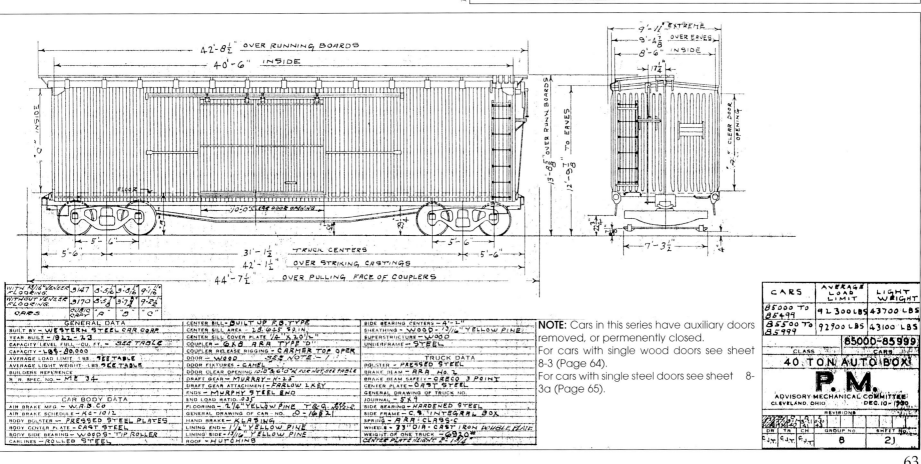

NOTE: Cars in this series have auxiliary doors removed, or permenently closed.
For cars with single wood doors see sheet 8-3 (Page 64).
For cars with single steel doors see sheet 8-3a (Page 65).

CARS	AVERAGE LOAD LIMIT	LIGHT WEIGHT
85000 TO 85499	92300 LBS	43700 LBS
85500 TO 85999	92900 LBS	43100 LBS

85000-85999

CLASS | CARS
40 TON AUTO BOX

P. M.
ADVISORY MECHANICAL COMMITTEE
CLEVELAND, OHIO · DEC. 10 · 1930

RENUMBERINGS

PM SERIES	FIRST APPEARED	DESCRIPTION
54000-54051	1945	Automotive Steering Gears
54100-54163	1945	Chevrolet Castings
54200-54240	1945	Chevrolet Bumpers
54500-54578	1946	
54570-54571	1949	
55001	1945	
55300-55309	1946	Equipped for Handling Gas-Oil Furnaces
55310-55319	1649	U. S. Radiator (Gas-Oil Furnaces)
55400-55407	1947	
69011-69018	1946	Insulated

ABOVE: PM No. 85908, a single-door conversion, is shown in 1941 at Los Angeles.

NOTE: Cars in this series equipped with Apex Tri-Lok metal running boards.

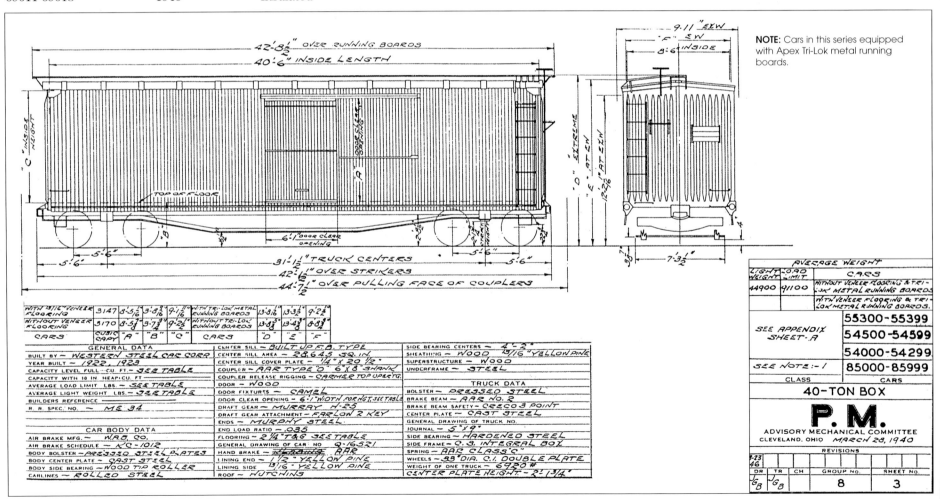

LEFT: Riding on Andrews replacement trucks, PM former auto car No. 85037 had its auxiliary door removed and the door opening reduced to 6'1" wide. Some of the single-door conversions retained their original wooden Camel doors as in this case. Others received Youngstown top hung steel doors from the 86000-87499 series, while still others were equipped with the Youngstown "bottom roller" steel auxiliary doors from series 89350-90349. No records exist to show which cars received which doors.

AVERAGE WEIGHT		
LIGHT WEIGHT	LOAD LIMIT	CARS
44900	10.80 91100	WITHOUT VENEER FLOORING & TRI-LOK METAL RUNNING BOARDS
		WITH VENEER FLOORING & TRI-LOK METAL RUNNING BOARDS

NOTE:-2 MAIN DOORS FROM 86000-87499 AND REBUILT AUXILIARY DOORS FROM 89350-90359. APPL. 10.

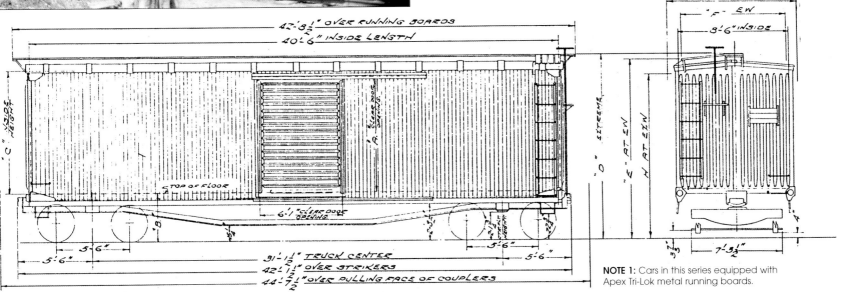

42'-8½" OVER RUNNING BOARDS
40'-6" INSIDE LENGTH
6'-1" CLEAR DOOR OPENING
31'-11½" TRUCK CENTER
42'-1½" OVER STRIKERS
44'-7½" OVER PULLING FACE OF COUPLERS
5'-6" 5'-6" 5'-6" 5'-6"
"C" HIGH   TOP OF FLOOR

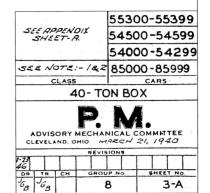

SXW
EW
8'-6" INSIDE
"F" EW
"E" AT EW
"H" AT SXW
"O" EXTREME
7'-5½"

NOTE 1: Cars in this series equipped with Apex Tri-Lok metal running boards.

WITH 13/16 VENEER FLOORING	3147	8'-5¼"	3'-8¾"	9'-1½"	WITH TRI-LOK METAL RUNNING BOARDS	13'-8½"	13'-3½"	9'-2½"	WITH MAIN DOORS FROM 86000-87499 SERIES	12'-3⁹⁄₁₆"	9'-9⁷⁄₈"
WITHOUT VENEER FLOORING	3170	8'-5¼"	3'-7¾"	9'-2¾"	WITHOUT TRI-LOK METAL RUNNING BOARDS	13'-5½"	13'-4¾"	8'-8¾"	WITH REBUILT AUX. DOORS FROM 89350-90349 SERIES	12'-0⁷⁄₆"	9'-10½"
CARS	CUBIC CAPY	A	B	C	CARS	D	E	F	CARS	H AT SXW	SZW

GENERAL DATA		
BUILT BY - WESTERN STEEL CAR CORP.	CENTER SILL - BUILT UP F.B. TYPE	SIDE BEARING CENTERS - 4'-2"
YEAR BUILT - 1922-1923	CENTER SILL AREA - 23.645 SQ. IN.	SHEATHING - 13/16" YELLOW PINE
CAPACITY LEVEL FULL CU. FT - SEE TABLE	CENTER SILL COVER PLATE - ¼" X 20½"	SUPERSTRUCTURE - WOOD
CAPACITY WITH 10 IN. HEAP CU. FT	COUPLER - AAR TYPE "D" 6"X8"	UNDERFRAME - STEEL
AVERAGE LOAD LIMIT LBS - SEE TABLE	COUPLER RELEASE RIGGING - CARMER TOP OPER'TG	
AVERAGE LIGHT WEIGHT LBS - SEE TABLE	DOOR - YOUNGSTOWN STEEL SEE NOTE:-2.	TRUCK DATA
BUILDERS REFERENCE	DOOR FIXTURES - CAMEL	BOLSTER - PRESSED STEEL
R.R. SPEC. NO - ME 34	DOOR CLEAR OPENING - 6'-1" W. SEE TABLE FOR HEIGHT	BRAKE BEAM - AAR NO. 2
	DRAFT GEAR - MURRAY H-25	BRAKE BEAM SAFETY - CRSCO 3 POINT
	DRAFT GEAR ATTACHMENT - FARLON 2 KEY	CENTER PLATE - CAST STEEL
CAR BODY DATA	ENDS - MURPHY 7/32 STEEL	GENERAL DRAWING OF TRUCK NO.
AIR BRAKE MFG - W.A.B. CO.	END LOAD RATIO - .035	JOURNAL - 5"X9"
AIR BRAKE SCHEDULE - KC 1012	FLOORING - 2¼" T&G SEE NOTE:-2	SIDE BEARING - HARDENED STEEL
BODY BOLSTER - PRESSED STEEL PLATES	GENERAL DRAWING OF CAR NO - Q-16521	SIDE FRAME - C.S. INTEGRAL BOX
BODY CENTER PLATE - CAST STEEL	HAND BRAKE - KLASING AAR	SPRING - AAR CLASS "C"
BODY SIDE BEARING - WOODS TIP ROLLER	LINING END - 1½" YELLOW PINE	WHEELS - 33" DIA. C.I. DOUBLE PLATE
CARLINES - ROLLED STEEL	LINING SIDE - 13/16" - YELLOW PINE	WEIGHT OF ONE TRUCK - 6920 *
	ROOF - HUTCHINS	CENTER PLATE HEIGHT - 2'-1¾"

SEE APPENDIX SHEET-A	55300-55399
	54500-54599
	54000-54299
SEE NOTE:-1&2	85000-85999
CLASS	CARS
40- TON BOX	

P. M.
ADVISORY MECHANICAL COMMITTEE
CLEVELAND, OHIO   MARCH 21, 1940

REVISIONS				
7-23-46				
DR JGB	TR JGB	CH	GROUP NO. 8	SHEET NO. 3-A

ABOVE: By the time this end view of PM No. 85250 was taken in August 1948, the Klasing hand brake had been replaced by a more standard AAR staff type brake wheel.

RIGHT: This view, apparently taken on the lot of Western Steel Car & Foundry in 1923, clearly shows the unusual steel end that was a hallmark of the 85000-series auto cars. Resembling something like a washboard, these Murphy ends consisted of two panels of vertical ribs joined at the center with a riveted seam. They must have been successful because the cars retained the ends throughout the various rebuildings. Another type of vertical-rib steel end of the era was the *Vulcan* end, which had fewer ribs of greater thickness, all protruding inward. The Chicago & North Western box cars in the photo are fitted with the more familiar Murphy 7/8 horizontal rib end. The Klasing ratchet-type hand brake was widely used by the PM in the 1920s.

These 1,500 40-foot auto cars were built by Pressed Steel Car Company in 1923 at a cost of approximately $3,180,000.00. They were nearly identical to the 85000-series, differing only in having steel doors and Hutchins ends. A note on the diagram says that 785 cars got their doors changed from top hung to bottom roller with Camel fixtures applied (see car No. 86975 on Page 69). All of these cars were converted to single-door by rebuilding or permanently closing the auxiliary doors in 1937-1943. Again, various cars were renumbered and equipped for special services. Renumbered cars from both groups were mixed indiscrimately as the railroad tended to treat both series as one big group.

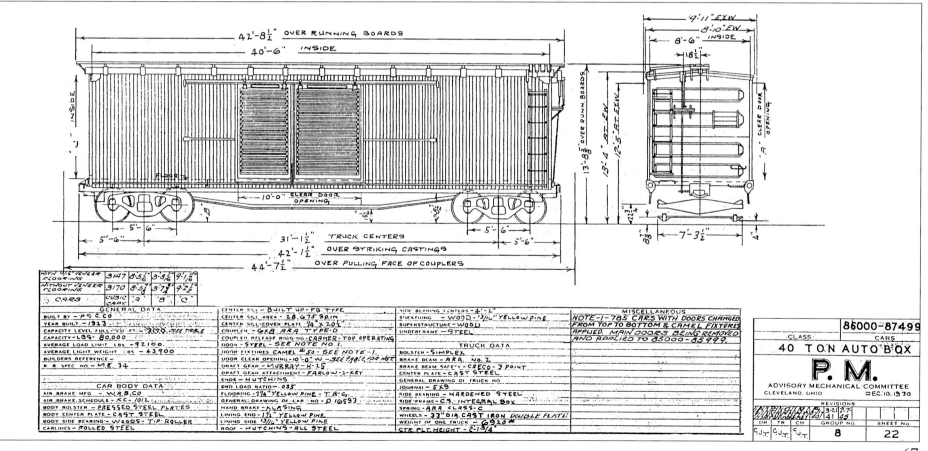

ABOVE: PM No. 86831, photographed at Grand Rapids on November 5, 1943, is unusual in that its double steel doors were replaced with a six-foot wooden door.

ABOVE: PM No. 86994, photographed at New London, Connecticut, in October 1948, is typical of cars from series 86000-87499 rebuilt with a six-foot door opening. It has retained its original steel main door (now converted with bottom rollers and a lower door track).

RIGHT: This end view of PM No. 86975, was taken at the same time as the side view on the opposite Page. The Hutchins steel end, manufactured in Detroit, was used extensively by the PM. Note the Klasing ratchet-type hand brake and the Carmer top-operating coupler lever.

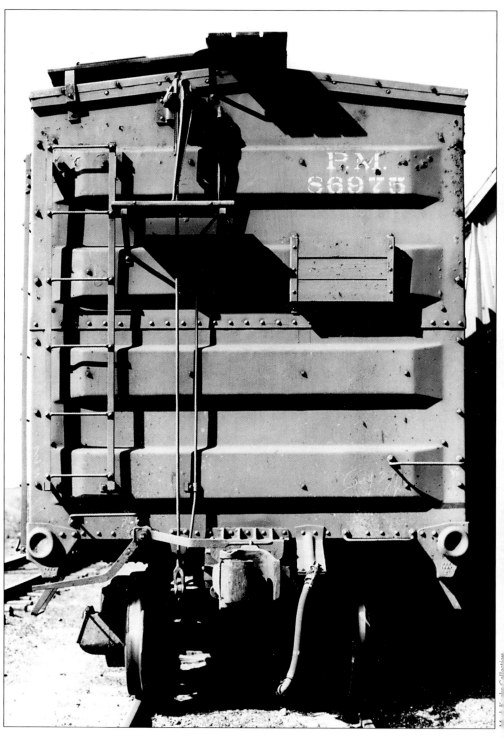

ABOVE: Built in May 1923 by Pressed Steel Car Company, PM Automobile and Furniture car No. 86975 was photographed at Dean Yard in Midland, Michigan, on June 19, 1930. The reweigh date "SAG 3-29" indicates a recent shopping at the Saginaw Shops, but the car is still in its original condition, featuring the double Youngstown corrugated steel doors. It has been modified with bottom rollers and lower door tracks for improved operation. By 1943, all of the cars in this series were converted to single-door cars by removing or, in some cases, permanently closing the auxiliary doors. The six-foot wide auxiliary doors removed from the 89350-90349 series (see Page 80) were rebuilt and applied to the converted cars. These were "bottom roller" doors and would have been an improvement over the original doors. As the original 86000-series doors were replaced, they were applied to cars in the 85000-series to replace the wood doors when they were converted to single-door cars.

PM SERIES	FIRST APPEARED	DESCRIPTION
54000-54051	1945	Automotive Steering Gear
54100-54163	1945	Chevrolet Castings
54200-54240	1945	Chevrolet Bumpers

NOTE:- 1
AUXILIARY DOORS REMOVED FROM 89,350-90,349 SERIES WERE REBUILT AND APPLIED.

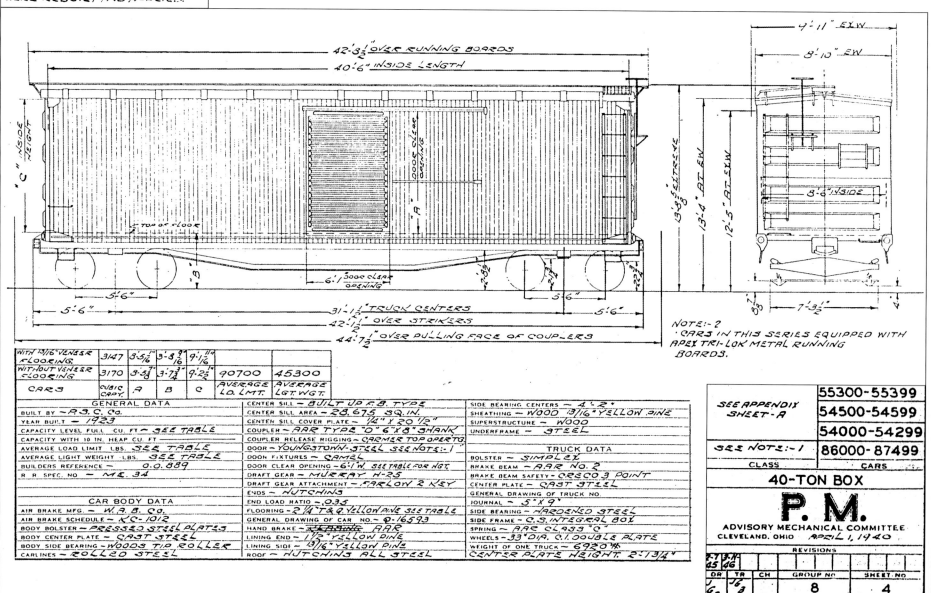

NOTE:- 2
CARS IN THIS SERIES EQUIPPED WITH APEX TRI-LOK METAL RUNNING BOARDS.

WITH 13/16" VENEER FLOORING	3147	3-5 1/16"	3-8 9/16"	9-1 11/16"			
WITHOUT VENEER FLOORING	3170	3-5 3/8"	3-7 3/8"	9-2 1/2"	90700	45300	
CARS	CUBIC CAP'Y.	A	B	C	AVERAGE LD. LMT.	AVERAGE LGT. WGT.	

GENERAL DATA
BUILT BY – P.S.C. Co.
YEAR BUILT – 1923
CAPACITY LEVEL FULL CU. FT – SEE TABLE
CAPACITY WITH 10 IN. HEAP CU. FT –
AVERAGE LOAD LIMIT LBS. SEE TABLE
AVERAGE LIGHT WEIGHT LBS. SEE TABLE
BUILDERS REFERENCE – O.O.889
R R SPEC. NO – ME.34

CAR BODY DATA
AIR BRAKE MFG. – W.A.B. Co.
AIR BRAKE SCHEDULE – KC-1012
BODY BOLSTER – PRESSED STEEL PLATES
BODY CENTER PLATE – CAST STEEL
BODY SIDE BEARING – WOODS TIP ROLLER
CARLINES – ROLLED STEEL

CENTER SILL – BUILT UP F.B. TYPE
CENTER SILL AREA – 28.675 SQ. IN.
CENTER SILL COVER PLATE – 1/4" X 20 1/2"
COUPLER – AAR TYPE "O" 6"X8" SHANK
COUPLER RELEASE RIGGING – CARMER TOP OPER'TG.
DOOR – YOUNGSTOWN-STEEL SEE NOTE:-1
DOOR FIXTURES – CAMEL
DOOR CLEAR OPENING – 6-1'W. SEE TABLE FOR HGT.
DRAFT GEAR – MURRAY H-25
DRAFT GEAR ATTACHMENT – FARLOW 2 KEY
ENDS – HUTCHINS
END LOAD RATIO – .035
FLOORING – 2 1/4" T&Q. YELLOW PINE SEE TABLE
GENERAL DRAWING OF CAR NO.~ Q-16593
HAND BRAKE – STAFFORD AAR
LINING END – 1 1/2" YELLOW PINE
LINING SIDE – 13/16" YELLOW PINE
ROOF – HUTCHINS ALL STEEL

SIDE BEARING CENTERS – 4-2"
SHEATHING – WOOD 13/16" YELLOW PINE
SUPERSTRUCTURE – WOOD
UNDERFRAME – STEEL

TRUCK DATA
BOLSTER – SIMPLEX
BRAKE BEAM – AAR NO. 2
BRAKE BEAM SAFETY – CRESCO 3 POINT
CENTER PLATE – CAST STEEL
GENERAL DRAWING OF TRUCK NO.
JOURNAL – 5"X 9"
SIDE BEARING – HARDENED STEEL
SIDE FRAME – C.S. INTEGRAL BOX
SPRING – AAR CLASS "C"
WHEELS – 33"DIA. C.I. DOUBLE PLATE
WEIGHT OF ONE TRUCK – 6920 #
CENTER PLATE HEIGHT. 2-13/4"

SEE APPENDIX SHEET-A

SEE APPENDIX SHEET-A	55300-55399
	54500-54599
	54000-54299
SEE NOTE:-1	86000-87499
CLASS	CARS

40-TON BOX

P.M.
ADVISORY MECHANICAL COMMITTEE
CLEVELAND. OHIO   APRIL 1, 1940

REVISIONS

DR	TR	CH	GROUP NO	SHEET.NO
J.H. 63	J.G. 63		8	4

This series of cars is remarkable in that they were built in Canada by National Steel Car Company for Pere Marquette "international" service and there is no notation of any of these cars ever undergoing a major rebuilding. In about 1934, the auxiliary doors on all of these cars were permanently sealed, giving the cars a six-foot wide door opening.

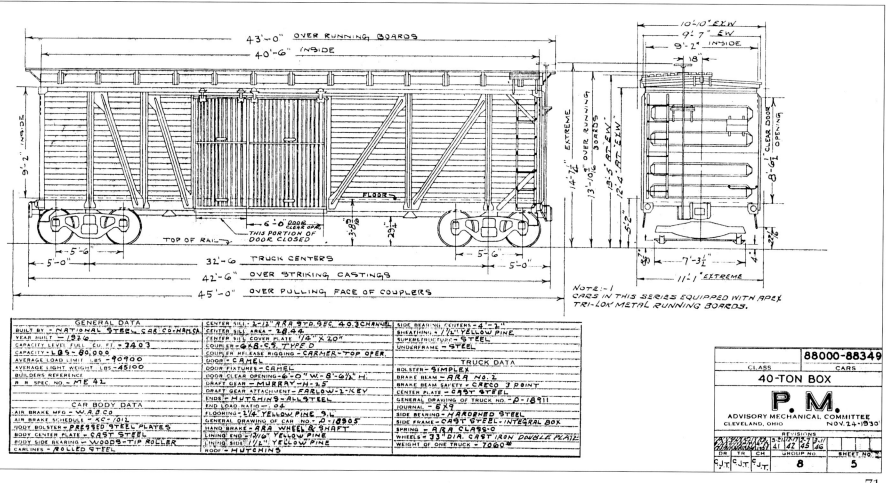

GENERAL DATA		
BUILT BY - NATIONAL STEEL CAR CO.-HAM.CA.	CENTER SILL - 2-12" ARA STD. SEC. 40.3 CHANNEL	SIDE BEARING CENTERS - 4'-2"
YEAR BUILT - 1926	CENTER SILL AREA - 28.44	SHEATHING - 1 1/2" YELLOW PINE
CAPACITY LEVEL FULL CU. FT. - 3403	CENTER SILL COVER PLATE 1/4" X 20"	SUPERSTRUCTURE - STEEL
CAPACITY LBS - 80,000	COUPLER - 6X8-C.S. TYPE D	UNDERFRAME - STEEL
AVERAGE LOAD LIMIT LBS - 90900	COUPLER RELEASE RIGGING - CARMER - TOP OPER.	
AVERAGE LIGHT WEIGHT LBS - 45100	DOOR - CAMEL	TRUCK DATA
BUILDERS REFERENCE	DOOR FIXTURES - CAMEL	BOLSTER - SIMPLEX
R R SPEC. NO - ME 42	DOOR CLEAR OPENING - 6'-0" W - 8'-6 1/2" H	BRAKE BEAM - ARA NO. 2
	DRAFT GEAR - MURRAY - H-25	BRAKE BEAM SAFETY - CRECO 3 POINT
	DRAFT GEAR ATTACHMENT - FARLOW-2-KEY	CENTER PLATE - CAST STEEL
CAR BODY DATA	ENDS - HUTCHINS - ALL STEEL	GENERAL DRAWING OF TRUCK NO. - P-18911
AIR BRAKE MFG - W.A.B.CO	END LOAD RATIO - .04	JOURNAL - 5 X 9
AIR BRAKE SCHEDULE - KC-1012	FLOORING - 2 1/4" YELLOW PINE 9L	SIDE BEARING - HARDENED STEEL
BODY BOLSTER - PRESSED STEEL PLATES	GENERAL DRAWING OF CAR NO. - P-18905	SIDE FRAME - CAST STEEL - INTEGRAL BOX
BODY CENTER PLATE - CAST STEEL	HAND BRAKE - ARA WHEEL & SHAFT	SPRING - ARA CLASS-O
BODY SIDE BEARING - WOODS-TIP ROLLER	LINING END - 1 7/16" YELLOW PINE	WHEELS - 33" DIA. CAST IRON DOUBLE PLATE
CARLINES - ROLLED STEEL	LINING SIDE - 1 1/2" YELLOW PINE	WEIGHT OF ONE TRUCK - 7060#
	ROOF - HUTCHINS	

88000-88349	
CLASS	CARS
40-TON BOX	

P. M.
ADVISORY MECHANICAL COMMITTEE
CLEVELAND, OHIO   NOV. 24-1930

REVISIONS				
		3-2-11 X 7 X 3-11		
		41	42	45	46

DR	TR	CH	GROUP NO.	SHEET NO.
C.J.T.	C.J.T.	C.J.T.	8	5

71

ABOVE: PM No. 88000 was built in Canada by National Steel Car Company in August 1926. This series of single-sheathed cars continued the use of the Hutchins steel ends, but the interior width was eight-inches wider than the 85000-87499 series of double-sheathed box cars built in 1922-23. The U-section exterior steel framing allowed the use of a straight center sill, whereas the wood-framed double-sheathed cars required the more substantial "fishbelly" center sill. Note the top-hung wooden doors and the T-section trucks.

LEFT: "I'll take 1,000 box cars," said the purchasing agent. - *Pere Marquette Service Magazine*, October 1927. Built by Pressed Steel Car Company in 1927, PM auto car No. 88700 is identical to the Canadian-built cars except for being equipped with an Ajax power hand brake and Dalman trucks. The Hutchins steel end was a Pere Marquette favorite.

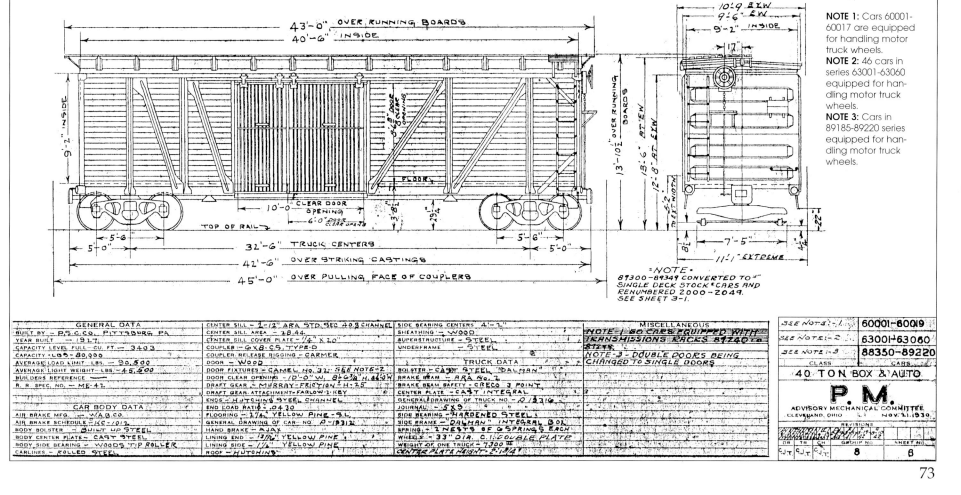

NOTE 1: Cars 60001-60017 are equipped for handling motor truck wheels.

NOTE 2: 46 cars in series 63001-63060 equipped for handling motor truck wheels.

NOTE 3: Cars in 89185-89220 series equipped for handling motor truck wheels.

This series can be considered the American counterpart to the previous (88000-88349) auto cars. A note on the diagram sheet states that cars 89185-89220 were having their double-doors replaced with single-doors, and were equipped for handling "motor wheel truck wheels." Most of the cars in this series were eventually converted to single-door cars (all 854 cars remaining in series 88350-89220 were listed as having six-foot door openings in the October 1941 *Equipment Register*). In 1934, the last 50 cars from this series, Nos. 89300-89349, were converted at the Wyoming Shops to stock cars 2000-2049 (see Page 36). In addition, cars from this series were reassigned, sometimes at random, to specific services, and were renumbered accordingly. Car No. 88958 survives at the Baltimore & Ohio Railroad Museum, in Baltimore, Maryland.

BELOW: PM No. 88987, in the most modern PM lettering style. The small lettering on the auxiliary door reads "Single Door Car," indicating it has been permanently closed.

RENUMBERINGS

PM SERIES	FIRST APPEARED	DESCRIPTION
54260-54274	1948	
54300-54348	1946	Chevrolet Transmissions
54600-54620	1946	Buick Transmissions
55100	1947	
60001-60014*	1937	Buick Transmissions
60015-60019	1937	Buick Transmissions

(PM 60001-60019 are believed to be ex-PM Nos. 89221-89239)

63001-63060*	1937	Chevrolet Transmissions

(PM 63001-63060 are believed to be ex-PM Nos. 89240-89299)

*These cars retained their ten-foot door openings.

ABOVE: Almost like new after being reconditioned at the Wyoming Shops, PM No. 54603 receives the last of its stenciling in the company of an un-rebuilt sister in September 1945. The auxiliary door on this car has been permanently sealed shut (note the "SINGLE DOOR" lettering and the lack of top rollers). The main door reads, "BKT RETURN WHEN EMPTY TO PM RY FLINT MICH."

THIS PAGE: The company photographer visited the Wyoming Shops at Grand Rapids in September 1945, and documented cars from PM series 88650-89220 being reconditioned and renumbered into the 54600-series for the transportation of Buick transmissions. Defective siding was replaced as needed, and other repairs were performed, including making the auxiliary doors inoperative. Already completed PM No. 54603 can be seen through the openings of box car No. 88746 above.

ABOVE: PM *Automobile and Furniture* car No. 89399 was built in June 1929 by Pressed Steel.

These 40-ton single-sheathed auto cars were built by Pressed Steel Car Company in 1929. Equipped with double Youngstown steel doors over a 12-foot door opening, Ajax power hand brakes, and Dalman trucks, they were the last wood sided automobile cars purchased by the Pere Marquette. This series of 1,000 cars was subjected to a variety of rebuildings over the years and, beginning in 1940, more than 800 were converted into single-door box cars. Some were rebuilt with new steel sides, roofs, and doors by the C&O beginning in 1951. Others had all of this done plus new ends, resulting in an entirely new car from the frame up. It's also known that some of the cars remained as-built with their double-doors intact. In addition to the various rebuildings, eventually 923 of the cars were renumbered in programs that continued into the 1950s under the C&O.

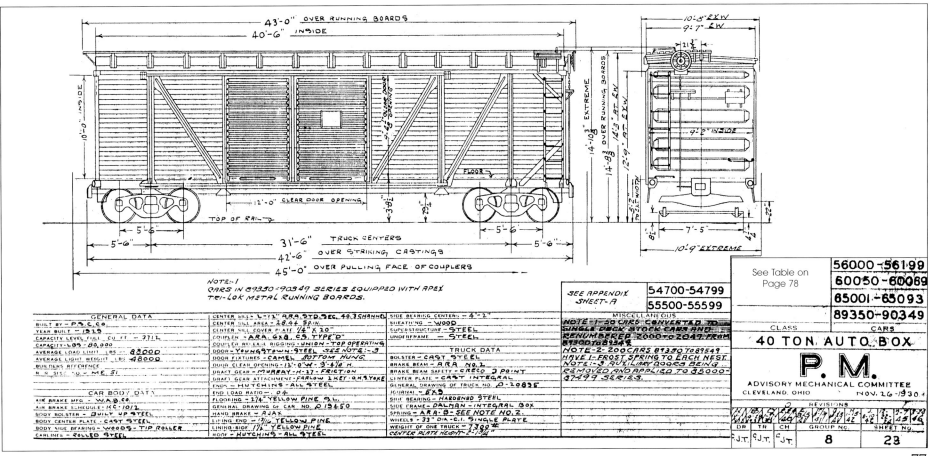

RENUMBERINGS

PM SERIES	FIRST APPEARED	DESCRIPTION
54045-54051	1948	
54055-54059	1949	
54155-54163	1948	
54240	1948	
54250-54254	1949	
54260-54274	1951	
54550	1947	
54700-54709	1946	Buick Bumpers
54800-54835	1950	
55200-55209	1946	American Seating Company
55500-55527*	1946	Fisher Body
55600-55694*	1949	
55750-55779*	1948	
56000-56014*	1948	Timken Axles
56100-56199*	1946	Timken Tandem Axles
56300-56316	1948	Refrigerator Compressor Units
60050-60059	1942	Oldsmobile Steering Gear
60060-60073	1948	Oldsmobile Steering Gear
64075-64084	1942	
65001-65061*	1937	Ford Hubcaps
65062-65069	1946	Ford Hubcaps
65070-65093	1949	Ford Hubcaps
68001-68049*	1938	Automobile Bodies
68050-68069	1941	

Retained 12-foot door openings

ABOVE: PM box car No. 68004, a former auto car from series 89350-90349, at Grand Ledge, Michigan, on February 15, 1942. This car was equipped for handling automobile bodies, but retained its 12-foot door openings.

ABOVE: Built by Pressed Steel Car Company in July 1929, PM auto car No. 89967 is still in its original condition, but has acquired the latest style of Pere Marquette lettering, including the use of reporting marks and AAR "lines." Last reweighed at the Wyoming Shops in July 1937, it probably received fresh paint and lettering at that time.

LEFT: PM No. 89530 has retained the use of its auxiliary door. Prior to being renumbered and assigned to special service, the 89350-90349 series was classified XAF for automobile and furniture loading. By October 1942, over 500 of the cars had been converted to single-door and assigned to general service. By the end of WWII, only 200 cars remained with 12-foot door openings.

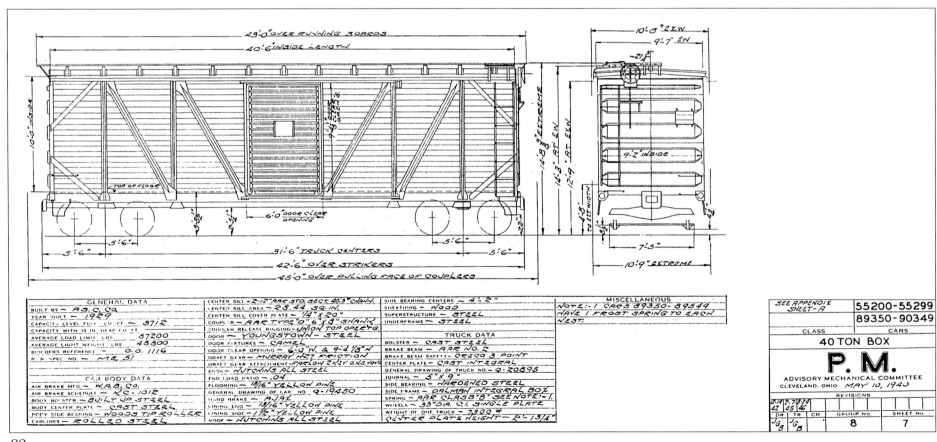

RIGHT: PM box car No. 90204 illustrates the appearance of the 89350-90349 series auto cars that were rebuilt to single-door beginning in 1940. This particular car was converted at the Wyoming Shops in March of that year. The auxiliary doors from these cars were removed and repaired, then used to upgrade double-sheathed cars in series 86000-87499 during their single-door conversions. The top hung six-foot steel doors removed from the 86000-series cars were in turn used to replace wood doors on cars converted in the 85000-85999 series. The Pere Marquette renumbered 96 of these 89350-series single-door rebuilds for auto parts service in the late-1940s. By the mid-1950s, there were nearly 130 cars assigned to auto parts service under C&O road numbers (see Page 147).

82000 - 83499

The 82000-series box cars are historically important because they were the first all-steel box cars on the Pere Marquette, arriving from Standard Steel Car Company in 1930. They also mark the beginning of the influence of the *Advisory Mechanical Committee* formed at that time. Remembered chiefly for its work in standardizing locomotives of the Erie, PM, Nickel Plate and C&O, the AMC also extended its research into other areas, including freight cars. This is an early example of that effort because the C&O had 1,500 nearly identical cars (series 8000-9499) and the Erie had 1,000 cars (series 75000-75999) of the same design.

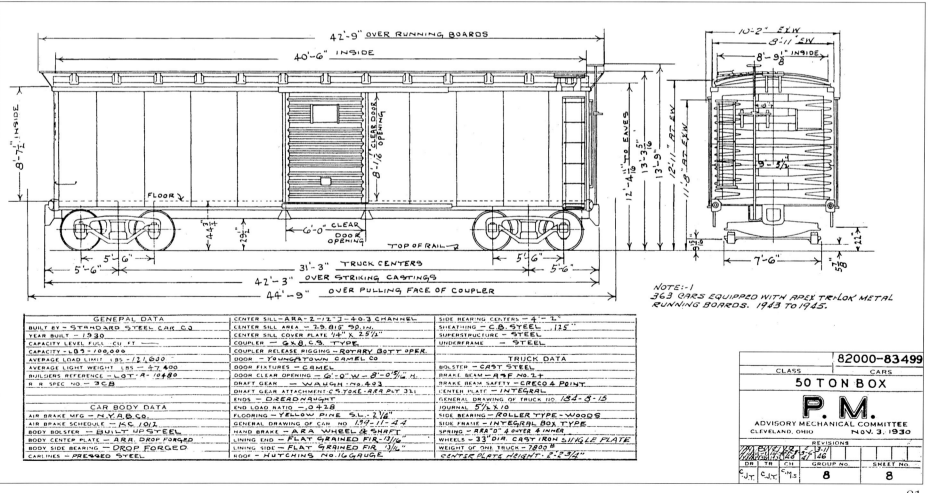

NOTE:-1
363 CARS EQUIPPED WITH APEX TRI-LOK METAL RUNNING BOARDS. 1943 TO 1945.

GENERAL DATA			
BUILT BY - STANDARD STEEL CAR CO	CENTER SILL - ARA-2-12"J-40.3 CHANNEL	SIDE BEARING CENTERS - 4'-2"	
YEAR BUILT - 1930	CENTER SILL AREA - 29.815 SQ.IN.	SHEATHING - C.B. STEEL .125"	
CAPACITY LEVEL FULL CU. FT	CENTER SILL COVER PLATE 14" X 25½"	SUPERSTRUCTURE - STEEL	
CAPACITY - LBS - 100,000	COUPLER - 6X8 C.S. TYPE	UNDERFRAME - STEEL	
AVERAGE LOAD LIMIT LBS - 121,600	COUPLER RELEASE RIGGING - ROTARY BOTT OPER.		
AVERAGE LIGHT WEIGHT LBS - 47,400	DOOR - YOUNGSTOWN CAMEL CO	TRUCK DATA	
BUILDERS REFERENCE - LOT-A-10480	DOOR FIXTURES - CAMEL	BOLSTER - CAST STEEL	
R R SPEC NO - 3CB	DOOR CLEAR OPENING - 6'-0" W - 8'-0⅝" H	BRAKE BEAM - ASF NO. 2+	
	DRAFT GEAR - WAUGH No. 403	BRAKE BEAM SAFETY - CRECO 4 POINT	
	DRAFT GEAR ATTACHMENT-C.S.YOKE-ARA PLT 321	CENTER PLATE - INTEGRAL	
CAR BODY DATA	ENDS - DREADNAUGHT	GENERAL DRAWING OF TRUCK NO. 184-8-15	
AIR BRAKE MFG - N.Y.A.B.CO.	END LOAD RATIO - .0428	JOURNAL 5½ X 10	
AIR BRAKE SCHEDULE - KC 1012	FLOORING - YELLOW PINE S.L. 2¼"	SIDE BEARING - ROLLER TYPE - WOODS	
BODY BOLSTER - BUILT UP STEEL	GENERAL DRAWING OF CAR NO 194-11-44	SIDE FRAME - INTEGRAL BOX TYPE	
BODY CENTER PLATE - ARA. DROP FORGED	HAND BRAKE - ARA WHEEL & SHAFT	SPRING - ARA "D" 4 OUTER 4 INNER	
BODY SIDE BEARING - DROP FORGED	LINING END - FLAT GRAINED FIR-13/16"	WHEELS - 33" DIA. CAST IRON SINGLE PLATE	
CARLINES - PRESSED STEEL	LINING SIDE - FLAT GRAINED FIR 13/16"	WEIGHT OF ONE TRUCK - 7800 #	
	ROOF - HUTCHINS No. 16 GAUGE	CENTER PLATE HEIGHT - 2'-2¾"	

82000-83499	
CLASS	CARS
50 TON BOX	

P. M.
ADVISORY MECHANICAL COMMITTEE
CLEVELAND, OHIO   NOV. 3, 1930

REVISIONS					
DR	TR	CH	GROUP NO.	SHEET NO.
C.J.T.	C.J.T.	C.M.S.	8	8

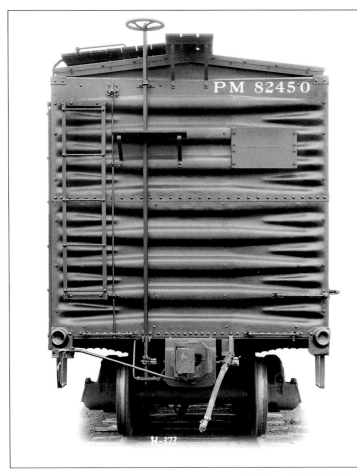

SSC Photo - Art Million Collection

ABOVE: Although the drawing on the diagram sheet shows a radial roof, the PM cars were actually delivered with Hutchins "peaked" roofs. Nearly identical cars built for the C&O and the Erie all received Climax radial roofs, and the diagram may reflect the original design intentions of the *Advisory Mechanical Committee* as it is essentially the same as the C&O's. The Hutchins roof, which was manufactured in Detroit, was used extensively by the PM. This two-piece "recessed" Dreadnaught steel end was applied to cars of this type purchased by the PM and the C&O from Standard Steel, and 500 of the Erie's cars, which came from Pressed Steel. The other 500 Erie cars were built by General American and were equipped with Buckeye steel ends.

ABOVE RIGHT: PM box car No. 83232 was built in August 1930 and was photographed in Washington D.C. in 1948 after having been upgraded with Apex metal running boards. The car still has KC brakes. These PM cars were built to the ARA 1923 all-steel box car design (similar to the PRR X-29) with an improved underframe layout, having the crossbearers positioned under the door posts, crossties between the crossbearers and bolsters, and the addition of single four-inch steel Z-section stringers. The most noticeable difference is the shorter truck center spacing (31'3" vs. 32'6") on the PM cars.

ABOVE: When PM No. 82472 was photographed on April 19, 1946, it had a second grabiron added to the left end of the side. These cars were never modified to any great extent by the PM. Compare the height of this car, and the Milwaukee Road single-sheathed car behind it, to that of the PRR auto car second from the end.

RENUMBERINGS

No car typifies the Pere Marquette more than the 50-foot double-door steel automobile car, and these represent the first of that type. Built by Pressed Steel Car company in 1930, they were also the only 50-footers with a staff hand brake. The major feature of these cars was the end doors on the A-end, which afforded obvious advantages in loading large objects and vehicles. As with so many other series of cars assigned to the automobile industry, these too underwent the usual renumberings and special assignments. In 1961, there were still 224 cars in service under C&O series 271000-271249. Some lasted until 1974.

PM SERIES	FIRST APPEARED	DESCRIPTION
59500-59529	1946	Fisher Body
59600-59611	1947	Timken Tandem Axles
59700-59727*	1947	
59728	1947	

Auxiliary door permanently closed.

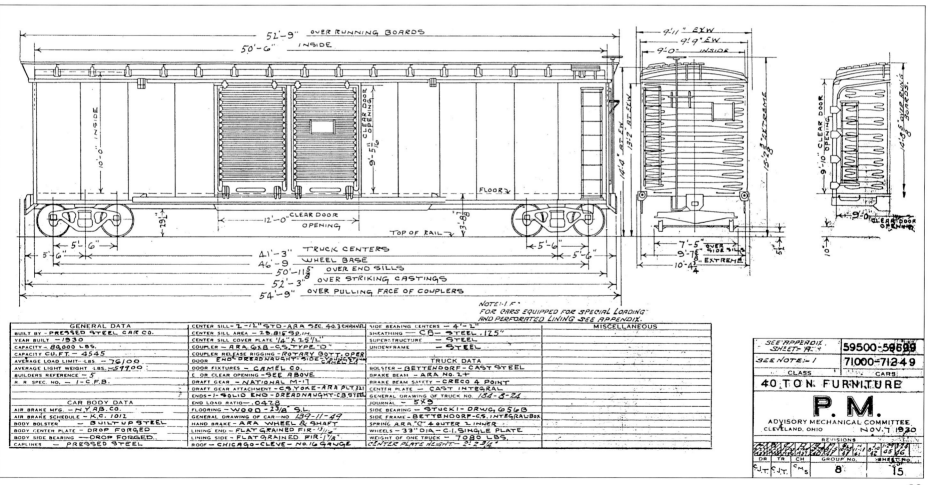

RIGHT: Close-up of the Bettendorf ARA truck with 33-inch diameter wheels as used under the 71000-series auto cars. Note the "PM RY" letters cast onto the side frame.

BELOW and OPPOSITE: Representing Pere Marquette's first all-steel 50-foot auto cars, PM No. 71249 was built in October 1930. The "bottom roller" Youngstown corrugated steel double-doors were the same as those applied to the 40-foot steel auto cars, series 90350-92349, also built in 1930. The 40-foot single-sheathed auto cars from series 89350-90349, built one year earlier, used these doors as well. All three car types had 12-foot door openings and a ten-foot interior height. The 50-footers were equipped with Dreadnaught end loading doors and Chicago-Cleveland Climax radial roofs, features shared with 500 of the steel 40-foot cars, numbers 91850-92349. The B-end was fitted with a three-piece steel "recessed" type Dreadnaught end with staff hand brakes (compare the end views, opposite, to those on Page 92).

85

This second order for 50-foot auto cars built in 1936 established the pattern for all subsequent orders for this type of car. They differed from the preceding series by having a wider door opening, in the use of power hand brakes, and by not having end doors. Within a few years, a number of cars received perforated steel linings. Again, some of these were renumbered upon assignment to specific industries.

RENUMBERINGS

PM SERIES	FIRST APPEARED
59750-59763	1947

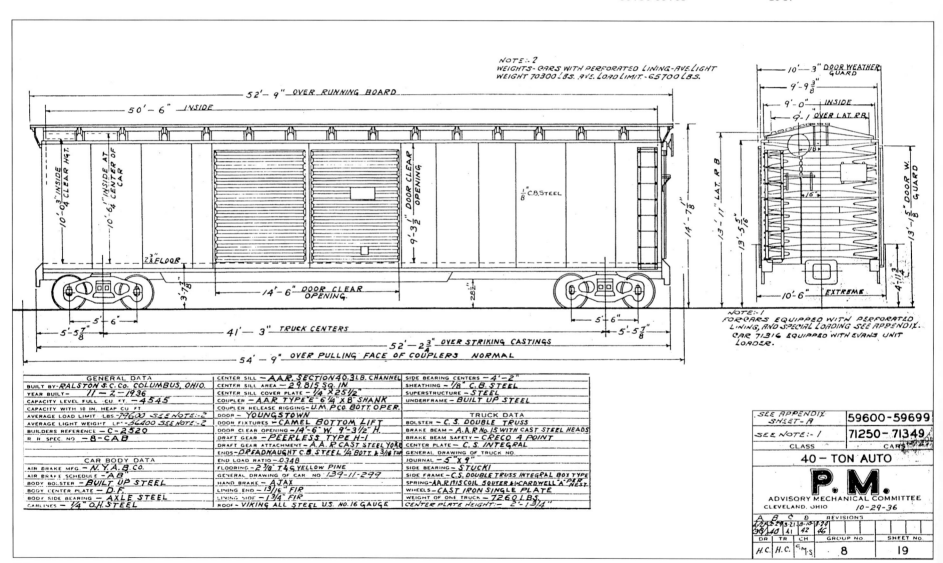

ABOVE: The Gould double-truss 40-ton truck used under the 71250-series auto cars.

LEFT: Fifty-foot auto car No. 71294, delivered in October 1936, was part of a group of 100 cars built for the PM by Ralston Steel Car Company in Columbus, Ohio. They had a 14'6" wide door opening for better side access, but came without end doors. The cars were fitted with Youngstown steel doors, Viking roofs, Dreadnaught ends, and Ajax power hand brakes. By this time, AB brakes had become standard equipment. Both of the PM's first two series of 50-foot auto cars had three-crossbearer underframes with single stringers, and U-section interior side posts.

LEFT : Pere Marquette 50-foot auto car No. 71253 was assigned to auto parts service and received a perforated steel interior lining (see Page 143) for restraining loads of auto parts, the work having been completed at the Wyoming Shops in December 1938. With the installation of the lining, the clear door opening was reduced to seven feet and the auxiliary doors were permanently closed. Due to the additional weight, the capacity was reduced to 65,000 lbs. By 1939, 60 of these 50-footers, PM Nos. 71250-71310, had been converted. Also, 12 cars, Nos. 71338-71349, were equipped with special racks for automobile axle loading. These too had seven-foot door openings. In 1940, cars 71317-71337 got perforated steel linings for a total of 81. In 1941, car No. 71316 was equipped with Evans Utility Loaders and cross-bars for shipping auto parts. In 1947, the 12 axle loading cars were renumbered to 56750-59763. All except car No. 59753 regained their original 14'6" door openings. By 1961, 90 cars with six-foot door openings were still in service under C&O series 271250-271349. Another six cars in this series were listed as having the 14'6" door opening. The last car with a PM road number was 59758.

ABOVE and RIGHT: The Pere Marquette's second series of 50-foot auto cars shared similar features to the 40-foot auto cars, series 93000-93399, built at the same time (see Page 94). They had two-piece "recessed" type Dreadnaught ends equipped with Ajax power hand brakes.

ABOVE: Pere Marquette auto car No. 91724 is equipped with Evans Type D auto loaders and has 16-floor tubes. It was last reweighed at Detroit in August 1939.

This large order for 2,000 cars was a shorter version of the 71000-series 50-foot auto car. These 40-foot cars were constructed in 1930 by two different builders. Pullman Car & Manufacturing Company delivered 1,500 cars, Nos. 90350-91849, while Pressed Steel Car Company built 500 cars, Nos. 91850-92349. The PSC cars were equipped with end loading doors and Chicago-Cleveland radial roofs. The Pullman cars lacked end doors and got Hutchins roofs. Pullman cars within the 90650-91849 number group received Evans Auto Loaders, some as early as 1933. The PSC cars with end doors were not so equipped. As a sidelight, in 1935, 100 cars (Nos. 90400-90499) were leased to the Chesapeake & Ohio Railway and were renumbered to that road's 6600-6699 series. They never returned to the Pere Marquette. Finally, a number of these cars were converted to single six-foot door cars by the C&O beginning in 1952.

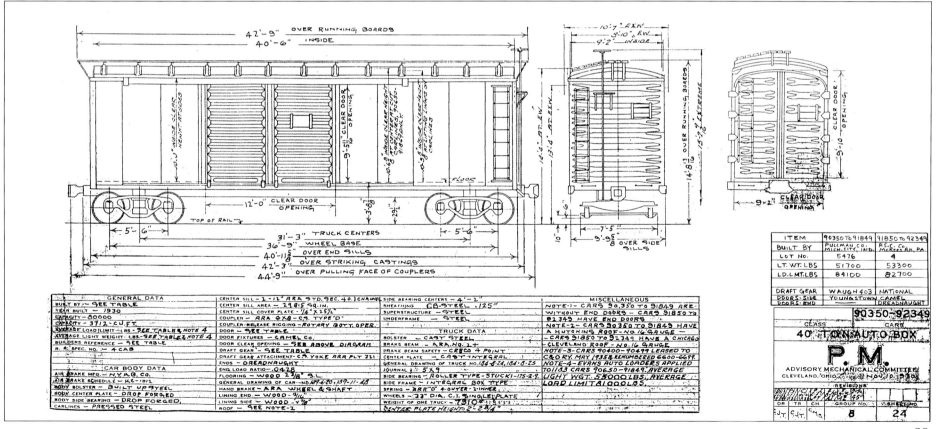

RIGHT: The transportation of automobiles warrented taller cars than what was required for shipping general merchandise and bulk commodities such as grain. That difference is nicely illustrated by PM auto car No. 91739, a ten-foot inside height car, coupled to PM box car No. 82807, which had an 8'7" inside height. Both were built in 1930. The PM auto cars of this period were rated at 40 tons, while the box cars had a 50-ton capacity.

BELOW: Pere Marquette 40-foot auto car No. 90991 posed for its official portrait in June 1930 at the Pullman plant in Michigan City, Indiana. By 1936, 1,000 cars, Nos. 90850-91849, were equipped with Evans auto loaders. In 1941, that number was increased by 200 cars, Nos. 90650-90849. The remaining cars did not get auto loaders, with 100 of these (90400-90488) having been leased to the C&O in 1935. In the 1950s, the C&O converted many of these cars to single six-foot door box cars in their 290350-291849 series (see Page 144). By 1961, there were still 298 cars on the roster with 12-foot doors, including 17 cars assigned to auto parts service and ten cars equipped for handling shipments of refrigerators.

ABOVE: Lumber being unloaded by Schweickart Lumber Company employees from PM No. 92134, at Ashland, Kentucky, sometime in the 1940s. The 500 Pressed Steel cars in series 91850-92349 featured Dreadnaught end doors, used primarily for loading large objects and vehicles such as trucks. Automobiles were normally loaded through the side doors.

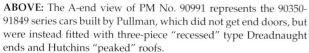

ABOVE: The A-end view of PM No. 90991 represents the 90350-91849 series cars built by Pullman, which did not get end doors, but were instead fitted with three-piece "recessed" type Dreadnaught ends and Hutchins "peaked" roofs.

TOP CENTER: Close examination of the B-end view of PM No. 92099 reveals the Chicago-Cleveland Climax radial roof fitted to PSC cars in series 91850-92349. All of the cars got staff hand brakes.

TOP RIGHT: The PM 40- and 50-foot auto cars built in 1930 shared construction features, particularly with regard to the Dreadnaught A-end loading doors.

RIGHT: Pressed Steel Car Company built PM No. 92099 in September 1930, part of a group of 500 such cars with end doors and radial roofs, series 91850-92349. Unlike their Pullman cousins, none of these cars were equipped with auto loaders or rebuilt to single-door cars. By 1961, 21 cars remained in the original PM series, while 449 cars had been renumbered to C&O series 291850-292349, 147 of which had their end doors welded shut.

93000 - 93399

These cars are distinguished by their 14-foot wide door openings. Built by Ralston Steel Car Company, all of the cars in this series were equipped with Evans Auto Loaders when new, as indicated by the white stripe on the car door.

LEFT: PM auto car No. 93162 was built in October 1936.

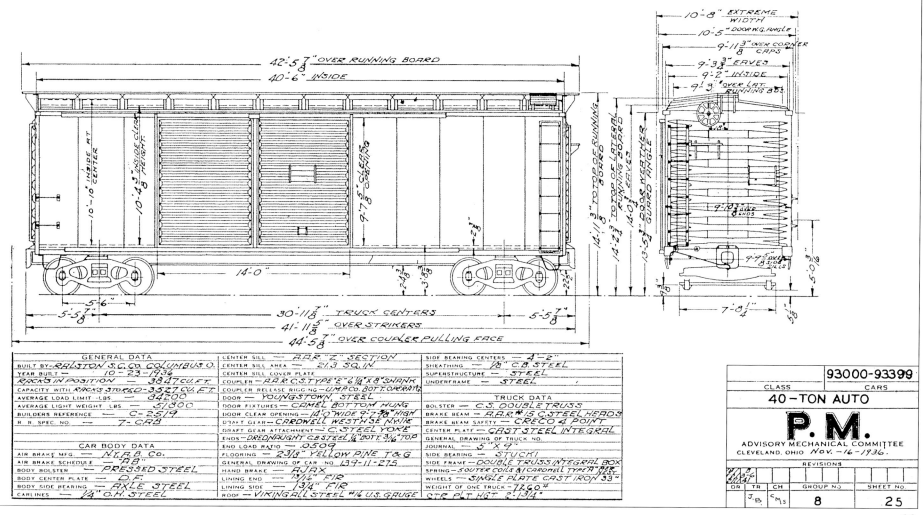

GENERAL DATA		CENTER SILL — A.A.R. "Z" SECTION	SIDE BEARING CENTERS — 4'-2"
BUILT BY — RALSTON S.C. Co. COLUMBUS O.		CENTER SILL AREA — 21.3 SQ. IN.	SHEATHING — 1/8" C.B. STEEL
YEAR BUILT — 10-23-1936		CENTER SILL COVER PLATE	SUPERSTRUCTURE — STEEL
RACKS IN POSITION — 3847 CU. FT.		COUPLER — A.A.R. C.S. TYPE "E" 6¼" X 8" SHANK	UNDERFRAME — STEEL
CAPACITY WITH RACKS STORED 3527 CU. FT.		COUPLER RELEASE RIGGING — U.M.P. Co. BOTT. OPERAT.	
AVERAGE LOAD LIMIT LBS. — 84200		DOOR — YOUNGSTOWN STEEL	TRUCK DATA
AVERAGE LIGHT WEIGHT LBS. — 51800		DOOR FIXTURES — CAMEL BOTTOM HUNG	BOLSTER — C.S. DOUBLE TRUSS
BUILDERS REFERENCE — C-2519		DOOR CLEAR OPENING — 14'-0" WIDE 9'-7 3/8" HIGH	BRAKE BEAM — A.A.R. #15 C. STEEL HEADS
R. R. SPEC. NO. — 7-CRB		DRAFT GEAR — CARDWELL WEST'H 50 NYIIE	BRAKE BEAM SAFETY — CRECO 4 POINT
		DRAFT GEAR ATTACHMENT — C. STEEL YOKE	CENTER PLATE — CAST STEEL INTEGRAL
CAR BODY DATA		ENDS — DREDNAUGHT C.B. STEEL 1/8" BOTT. 3/16" TOP	GENERAL DRAWING OF TRUCK NO.
AIR BRAKE MFG. — N.Y.A.B. Co.		END LOAD RATIO — .0509	JOURNAL — 5" X 9"
AIR BRAKE SCHEDULE — "AB"		FLOORING — 2 3/8" YELLOW PINE T&G	SIDE BEARING — STUCKI
BODY BOLSTER — PRESSED STEEL		GENERAL DRAWING OF CAR NO. 139-11-275	SIDE FRAME — DOUBLE TRUSS INTEGRAL BOX
BODY CENTER PLATE — D.F.		HAND BRAKE — AJAX	SPRING — 5 OUTER COILS & 1 CARDWELL TYPE "B" INR.
BODY SIDE BEARING — AXLE STEEL		LINING END — 13/16" FIR	WHEELS — SINGLE PLATE CAST IRON 33"
CARLINES — 1/4" O.H. STEEL		LINING SIDE — 13/4" FIR	WEIGHT OF ONE TRUCK — 7260 #
		ROOF — VIKING ALL STEEL #16 U.S. GAUGE	STR. PL'T HG'T 3'-13/4"

93000-93399	
CLASS	CARS
40-TON AUTO	

P.M.

ADVISORY MECHANICAL COMMITTEE
CLEVELAND, OHIO NOV. -16-1936.

REVISIONS				
DR	TR	CH	GROUP NO.	SHEET NO.
J.B.	C.M.S		8	25

ABOVE and BELOW: The two-piece "recessed" Dreadnaught ends on the 93000-series auto cars were identical to those fitted to the 50-foot auto cars of 1936. The cars also got Ajax power hand brakes and wood running boards.

ABOVE: Pere Marquette auto car No. 93368 was delivered in October 1936 with black-painted doors, ends, underframe, and trucks. Evans auto loaders were standard equipment for cars in this series, which were basically a short version of the 50-foot auto cars in series 71250-71349, all built by Ralston Steel. Similar features included Viking roofs and AB brakes. The Youngstown corrugated steel double-doors, although essentially the same as those on the 50-foot cars, were slightly narrower due to the 14-foot clear door opening of the 40-foot cars (the 50-footers had a 14'6" door opening).

RIGHT: These cars rode on Symington-Gould 40-ton double truss trucks with integral journal boxes.

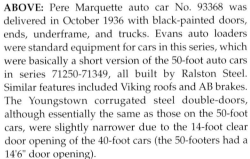

ABOVE: By the time PM No. 93179 was photographed about 1958, it had its auto loaders removed at the Wyoming Shops (September 1954), and was being used in general service. In 1954, there were still 397 of the original cars still in service, with 122 of those renumbered into C&O series 293000-293399. Cars that retained the use of their auto loaders included 90 cars from the 93000-series and 104 cars from the 293000-series. By 1961, only 24 general service cars remained in the 93000-series, but 362 cars from the 293000-series continued to be listed in various capacities, including 90 cars with auto loaders, 229 general service cars, and 43 cars assigned to auto parts shipments.

Evans Auto Loaders

The Pere Marquette, in conjunction with the Evans Products Company of Detroit, pioneered in the development of loading racks for the shipment of automobiles. Several different types were used, but all followed the same basic idea. The Evans Auto Loader was a system of racks installed inside a car of increased interior height. Attached to the top of the inner sides of the car, it allowed autos to be loaded, then lifted up and secured by a system of steel support rods and tie-downs. Floor tubes held the tie-down chains and springs when the racks were not in use. More autos could then be fitted into the remaining space beneath the suspended autos. Using these racks, four autos could be shipped in a single 40-foot auto car.

The installation of auto loaders in 40-foot Pere Marquette box cars began in 1933. About 1,700 cars from series 90650-93499 were eventually so equipped.

Some cars had their racks replaced with newer, improved model racks (see table). The photos show a Type E rack in car 90678 in 1948. The photo on the left shows the rack lowered and ready to receive an auto, while the view on the right shows the same rack in its fully raised or stored position. In actual use, the racks would be positioned somewhere between these extremes.

Initially, these Evans Auto Loaders were only installed in 40-foot cars. The C&O eventually installed racks in fifty ex-PM 50-foot cars. During World War II, while automobile production in the United States was curtailed, the Pere Marquette removed the racks from most of its cars, freeing them for the shipment of war-related goods flowing out of Detroit. The racks were re-installed following the resumption of auto production at the war's end. Auto Loader equipped cars are identified by a white stripe across the right-hand door.

Roth: Phil Schuster Collection

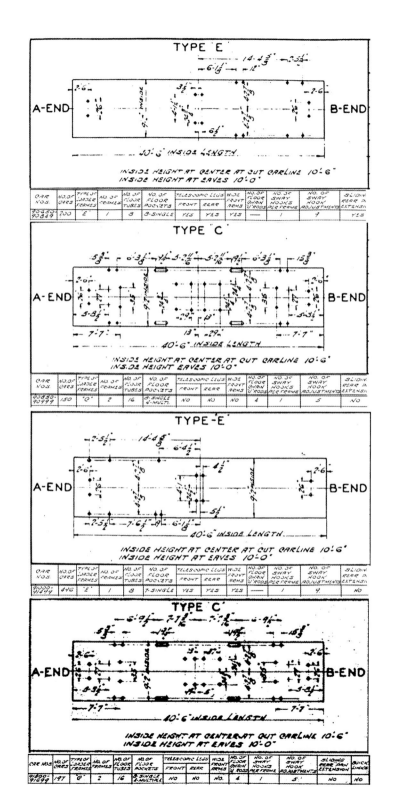

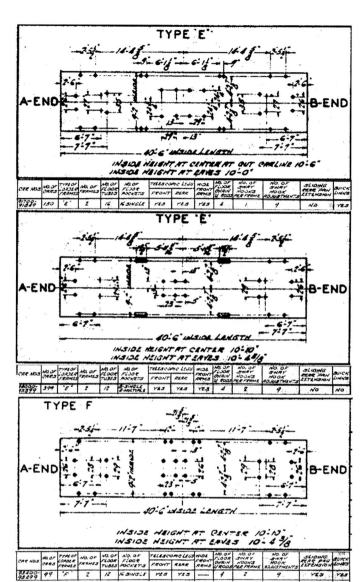

Pere Marquette
Floor Tube
Diagrams

PERE
MARQUETTE

3 The Modern Era

What we have termed as the Modern Era in our arbitrary breakdown of Pere Marquette freight car history, includes the last ten years of the PM's life as a separate corporation. This span covers World War II, when even more cars were added to the PM fleet to help handle the volume of war material issuing forth from Detroit, the "Arsenal of Democracy." There was no time for experimentation . . . tried-and-true designs were reordered and put to work immediately. Only one entirely new type of car appeared, first ordered before the outbreak of hostilities. This was the covered hopper car, built to handle the growing cement and bulk materials trade. The rebuilding programs continued and new ones were begun. These continued to the end, and even beyond, as many were simply taken over by the Chesapeake & Ohio and went on as if the merger had never taken place. Of course, it had, and the cars emerging reflected that fact with new C&O lettering and numbers. After June 6, 1947, the Pere Marquette began to disappear, piece by piece. Not only were locomotives repainted and renumbered, but freight cars were too. Of course, all this activity was dependent on the expiration of equipment trusts, but little by little, one car at a time, they began to go, until by the mid-1970s, they were all gone, save for a few placed in museums around the country.

The Chesapeake & Ohio system for renumbering former Pere Marquette cars was a simple one. Most of the former PM cars retained their original numbers, but the extra digit "2" preceded them. For example, a 50' auto car formerly PM 72125 would become C&O 272125. The most notable exceptions were PM stock cars 2000-2049, which became C&O 95300-95349.

PERE MARQUETTE

20000 - 20024 (2nd)

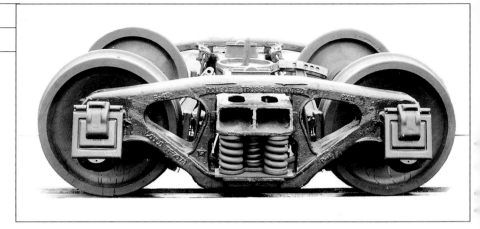

In 1937, the American Car and Foundry Company developed a standardized design for a 70-ton covered hopper, which proved to be so successful that it was duplicated with only minor variations for the next 20 years. Many thousands of these cars were sold to scores of American railroads as well as to private owners. The Pere Marquette joined the ranks in 1942 with a modest order for 25 cars.

RIGHT: The double-truss trucks beneath PM covered hoppers Nos. 20000-20024 came with wrought-steel wheels, instead of the steel castings previously used.

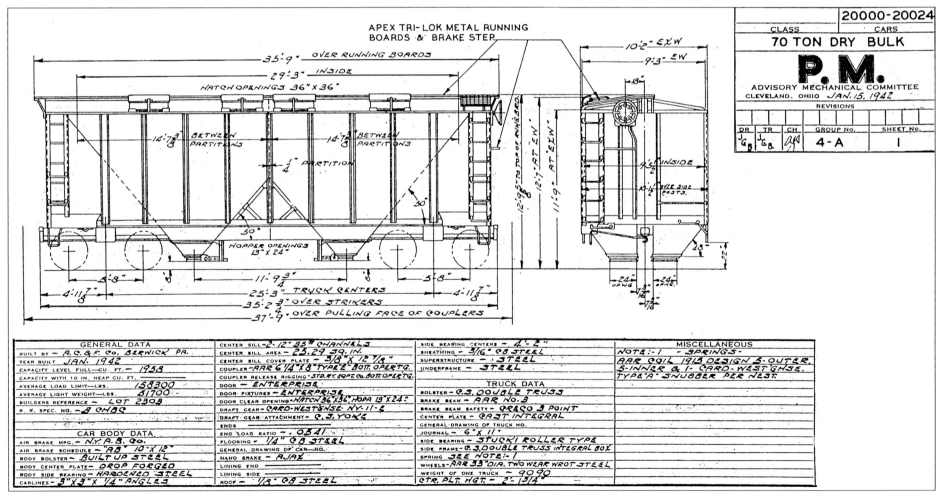

20000-20024	
CLASS	CARS
70 TON DRY BULK	
P.M.	
ADVISORY MECHANICAL COMMITTEE	
CLEVELAND, OHIO JAN. 15, 1942	

	GENERAL DATA	
BUILT BY	A.C. & F. CO. BERWICK PA.	
YEAR BUILT	JAN. 1942	
CAPACITY LEVEL FULL—CU. FT.	1958	
CAPACITY WITH 10 IN. HEAP CU. FT.		
AVERAGE LOAD LIMIT—LBS.	158300	
AVERAGE LIGHT WEIGHT—LBS.	51700	
BUILDERS REFERENCE	LOT 2308	
R. H. SPEC. NO.	9 CHBC	

CAR BODY DATA	
AIR BRAKE MFG.	N.Y.A.B. CO.
AIR BRAKE SCHEDULE	"AB" 10"X 12"
BODY BOLSTER	BUILT UP STEEL
BODY CENTER PLATE	DROP FORGED
BODY SIDE BEARING	HARDENED STEEL
CARLINES	3"X3"X 1/4" ANGLES

CENTER SILL	2-12"35# CHANNELS	
CENTER SILL AREA	23.29 SQ. IN.	
CENTER SILL COVER PLATE	3/8"X 12 7/8"	
COUPLER	AAR 6 1/4"X8"TYPE "E" BOTT. OPER'TG.	
COUPLER RELEASE RIGGING	STD. RY. EQPT CO. BOTT. OPER'TG.	
DOOR	ENTERPRISE	
DOOR FIXTURES	ENTERPRISE	
DOOR CLEAR OPENING	HATCH 36"X36", HOPR 13"X24"	
DRAFT GEAR	CARD-WEST'SE. NY.-11-E	
DRAFT GEAR ATTACHMENT	C. S. YOKE	
ENDS		
END LOAD RATIO	.0341	
FLOORING	1/4" CB STEEL	
GENERAL DRAWING OF CAR	NO.	
HAND BRAKE	AJAX	
LINING END		
LINING SIDE		
ROOF	1/8" CB STEEL	

	TRUCK DATA	
SIDE BEARING CENTERS	4'-2"	
SHEATHING	3/16" CB STEEL	
SUPERSTRUCTURE	STEEL	
UNDERFRAME	STEEL	
BOLSTER	C.S. DOUBLE TRUSS	
BRAKE BEAM	AAR NO. 3	
BRAKE BEAM SAFETY	QRASO 3 POINT	
CENTER PLATE	CAST INTEGRAL	
GENERAL DRAWING OF TRUCK NO.		
JOURNAL	6"X 11"	
SIDE BEARING	STUCKI ROLLER TYPE	
SIDE FRAME	C.S. DOUBLE TRUSS INTEGRAL BOX	
SPRING	SEE NOTE:-1	
WHEELS	AAR 33"DIA. TWO WEAR WROT STEEL	
WEIGHT OF ONE TRUCK	9090	
CTR. PLT. HGT.	2'- 13/4"	

MISCELLANEOUS
NOTE:-1 - SPRINGS- AAR COIL 1913 DESIGN 5-OUTER, 5-INNER & 1- CARD-WEST'GHSE. TYPE "A" SNUBBER PER NEST.

100

ABOVE: Pere Marquette covered hopper No. 20021 was built in January 1942 by AC&F at Berwick, Pennsylvania. This publicity view shows the car outlined in white, preparatory to "masking" out the background, with rather attractive results. These 70-ton cars had two separate compartments with four loading hatches and double discharge hoppers per bay. Note the *cement line* stencil at the top of the third panel from the left.

ABOVE: The construction details and stenciling are evident in these masked end views of PM covered hopper No. 20021. All 25 cars came with Apex Tri-Loc metal running boards, Ajax power hand brakes, and AB brake components.

LEFT and BELOW: Although PM Nos. 20000-20024 were never modified as a series, car No. 20011 was singled out for a remarkable rebuilding. What is so unusual about 20011 is that the date of rebuilding was June 1955, yet she remained lettered for the Pere Marquette. The work was done at the Wyoming Shops with the 20011 receiving a new roof with round hatches and modified discharge doors for calcium carbide loading. The rebuilt car was assigned to the Union Carbide Corporation.

PERE MARQUETTE

20025 - 20049 (2nd)

Pere Marquette's second order for another 25 AC&F covered hoppers followed the initial order, two years later. Except for minor weight differences, they were identical. The cars in this series were not modified during their lives as Pere Marquette cars (one car, C&O 220039, was modified for calcium carbide loading in the same program as PM No. 20011).

RIGHT: PM covered hopper No. 20049 was built in September 1944, about the time all-steel freight cars were allowed back in production by the War Production Board.

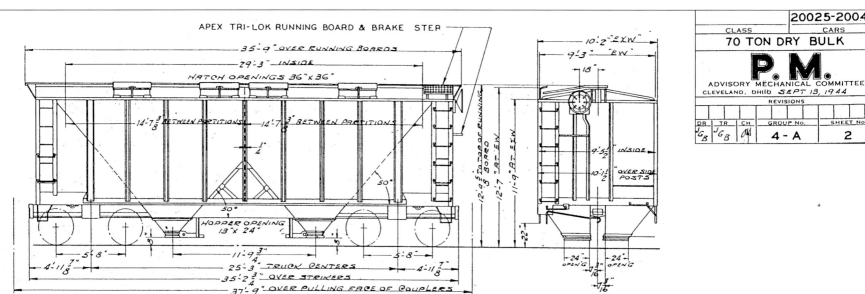

RIGHT: Builder's photo of Pere Marquette covered hopper No. 20049. Shown are the end and roof details common to this series built by AC&F at Madison, Illinois. Features include Apex steel running boards and brake step, eight loading hatches, Ajax power hand brake, and Westinghouse AB brakes. The earlier 20000-20024 series received New York AB brakes.

Below: Double-truss trucks used on series 200025-20049.

PERE MARQUETTE

20050 - 20149 (2nd)

Pere Marquette's third and final order for covered hoppers came in 1946, two years after the previous purchase. This time, 100 cars were ordered from Greenville Steel Car Company. Although they came from a different builder, they were virtually identical to previous cars. Minor differences include the use of U.S. Gypsum Company running boards and brake steps, instead of the Apex type used on the AC&F cars. Again, there were never any modifications to any of these cars while they were lettered PM.

RIGHT: Pere Marquette covered hopper No. 20050 was built in March 1946. These cars from Greenville Steel were near duplicates of the PM's AC&F products, but rode on A-3 Ride Control trucks.

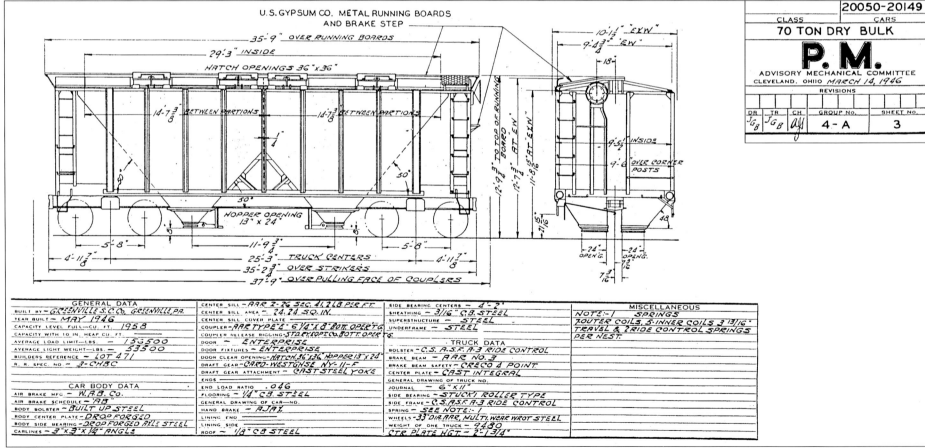

LEFT: The Pere Marquette's covered hopper cars survived in their original lettering longer than any other type of PM freight equipment. This photograph of PM No. 20091 was taken sometime after 1972, in the Chessie System era.

BELOW: Still lettered for the Pere Marquette, this car never carried C&O lettering. It's on display at the B&O Railroad Museum in Baltimore, Maryland.

16300-16319 (2nd)

Very little is known about the 20 Pere Marquette flat cars in this series. Products of the Wyoming Shops in 1943, they appear to have been rebuilt from former 80000-series USRA box cars with partial Hutchins end panels from 88000 or 89000-series auto cars that were narrowed and applied. The entire car body was removed from the underframe, then "fishbelly" side frames were applied to the side sills to provide additional floor strength, thus forming a 40-foot platform. A small bulkhead area was created at the ends by welding bars to the side frames and the end panels. Perhaps these cars were built for a specific service. All 20 cars were still in service at the end of WWII, but by early 1946, only nine were left. Most of these lasted into the C&O merger and were finally removed from service in 1953.

ABOVE: Rebuilt PM flat car No. 16300 carries a shop stencil of WY 11-43. Note that the poling pocket (which has been moved in-board), stirrup steps, Carmer top-operated coupler release lever, and Andrews trucks are common to the 80000-series USRA box cars. Except for the trucks, these features were also found on the 85000 and 86000-series auto cars, but the method of mounting the coupler release lever is peculiar to the USRA cars.

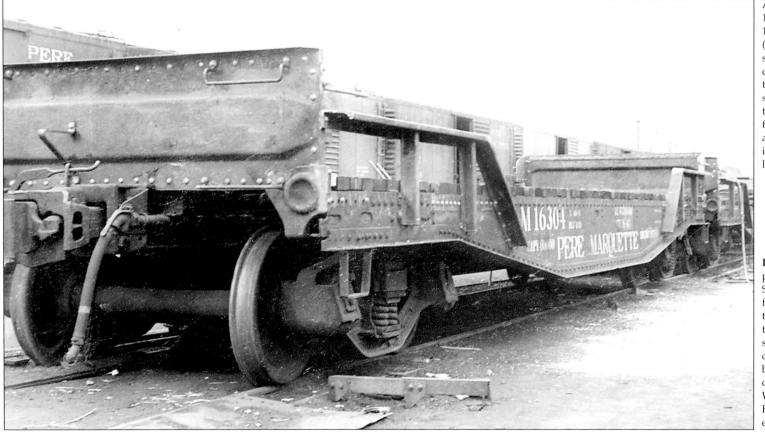

LEFT: PM flat car No. 16304 was photographed at the Wyoming Shops. The origin of these rebuilt flat cars is difficult to determine, but this view shows the "fishbelly" center sill of an 80000, 85000, or 86000-series double-sheathed box/auto car. The trucks have integral journal boxes and are similar to those found on the 85000 and 86000-series cars. While the 86000-series cars did have Hutchins ends, they were of a different rib style than these (see Page 68).

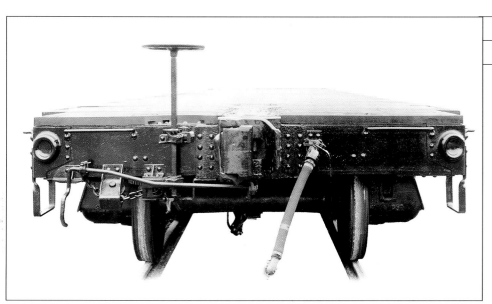

Though built two years apart, in 1942 and 1944, these two series of 70-ton flat cars can be considered as one, as the Pere Marquette did. All of the cars were built by the Greenville Steel Car Company and, except for slight variations, were nearly identical. Curiously, half of the cars from the first order, Nos. 16500-16624, had Westinghouse air brakes and Miner draft gear, while Nos. 16625-16749 had New York air brakes and Westinghouse draft gear. The final 100 cars, 16750-16849, reverted to the Westinghouse brakes, and had Waugh draft gear.

LEFT: The end view of PM flat car No. 16691 reveals the Equipco drop shaft hand brake that cars in series 16500-16749 were delivered with. These were not power-type brakes. The 16750-16849 series got Universal drop shaft power hand brakes. Note that the deck is notched for the drop brake wheel, and at the corners for personnel boarding.

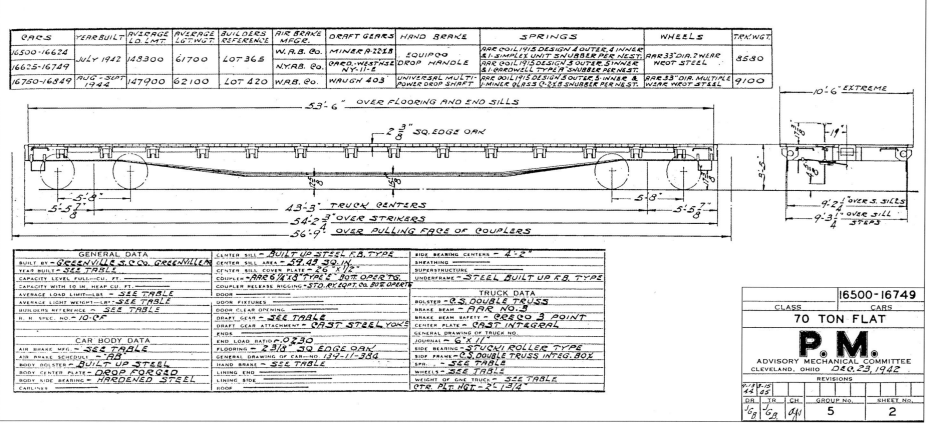

CARS	YEAR BUILT	AVERAGE LD. LMT.	AVERAGE LGT. WGT.	BUILDERS REFERENCE	AIR BRAKE MFGR.	DRAFT GEARS	HAND BRAKE	SPRINGS	WHEELS	TRK. WGT.
16500-16624	JULY 1942	148300	61700	LOT 365	W. A. B. Co.	MINER A-22-B	EQUIPCO DROP HANDLE	AAR COIL 1915 DESIGN 4 OUTER, 4 INNER &1-SIMPLEX UNIT SNUBBER PER NEST.	AAR 33" DIA. 2 WEAR WROT STEEL	8580
16625-16749					N.Y. R.B. Co.	CARD.-WESTNSE. N.Y.-11-E		AAR COIL 1915 DESIGN 5 OUTER, 5 INNER &1-CARDWELL TYPE A SNUBBER PER NEST.		
16750-16849	AUG.-SEPT. 1944	147900	62100	LOT 420	W.A.B. Co.	WAUGH 403	UNIVERSAL MULTI-POWER DROP SHAFT	AAR COIL 1915 DESIGN 5 OUTER, 5 INNER & 1 MINER CLASS C-2-B SNUBBER PER NEST.	AAR 33" DIA. MULTIPLE WEAR WROT STEEL	9100

53'-6" OVER FLOORING AND END SILLS

2 3/8" SQ. EDGE OAK

10'-6" EXTREME

5'-8"
5'-5 7/8"

13'-3" TRUCK CENTERS
54'-2 3/4" OVER STRIKERS
56'-9" OVER PULLING FACE OF COUPLERS

5'-8"
5'-5 7/8"

9'-2 1/4" OVER S. SILLS
9'-3 1/4" OVER SILL STEPS

GENERAL DATA			
BUILT BY - GREENVILLE S. C. Co. GREENVILLE PA.	CENTER SILL - BUILT UP STEEL F.B. TYPE	SIDE BEARING CENTERS - 4'-2"	
YEAR BUILT - SEE TABLE	CENTER SILL AREA - 59.43 SQ. IN.	SHEATHING	
CAPACITY LEVEL FULL---CU. FT.	CENTER SILL COVER PLATE - 26" X 1/2"	SUPERSTRUCTURE	
CAPACITY WITH 10 IN. HEAP CU. FT.	COUPLER - AAR 6 1/4" X 8" TYPE 'E' BOT. OPER'TG.	UNDERFRAME - STEEL BUILT UP F.B. TYPE	
AVERAGE LOAD LIMIT-LBS - SEE TABLE	COUPLER RELEASE RIGGING - STO. RY. EQPT. Co. BOT. OPER'TG.		
AVERAGE LIGHT WEIGHT-LBS - SEE TABLE	DOOR	TRUCK DATA	
BUILDERS REFERENCE - SEE TABLE	DOOR FIXTURES	BOLSTER - C.S. DOUBLE TRUSS	
R. R. SPEC. NO.- 10-CF	DOOR CLEAR OPENING	BRAKE BEAM - AAR NO. 3	
	DRAFT GEAR - SEE TABLE	BRAKE BEAM SAFETY - CRECO 3 POINT	
	DRAFT GEAR ATTACHMENT - CAST STEEL YOKE	CENTER PLATE - CAST INTEGRAL	
CAR BODY DATA	ENDS	GENERAL DRAWING OF TRUCK NO.	
AIR BRAKE MFG. - SEE TABLE	END LOAD RATIO - .0230	JOURNAL - 6" X 11"	
AIR BRAKE SCHEDULE - 'AB'	FLOORING - 2 3/8" SQ. EDGE OAK	SIDE BEARING - STUCKI ROLLER TYPE	
BODY BOLSTER - BUILT UP STEEL	GENERAL DRAWING OF CAR-NO. 139-11-384	SIDE FRAME - C.S. DOUBLE TRUSS INTEG. BOX	
BODY CENTER PLATE - DROP FORGED	HAND BRAKE - SEE TABLE	SPR. - SEE TABLE	
BODY SIDE BEARING - HARDENED STEEL	LINING END	WHEELS - SEE TABLE	
CARLINES	LINING SIDE	WEIGHT OF ONE TRUCK - SEE TABLE	
	ROOF	CTR. PLT. HGT. - 2'-13/4"	

16500-16749	
CLASS	CARS
70 TON FLAT	

P.M.
ADVISORY MECHANICAL COMMITTEE
CLEVELAND, OHIO   DEC. 23, 1942

REVISIONS

9-13 44	3-15 45					
DR	TR	CH	GROUP No.		SHEET No.
J.G.B.	J.G.B.	A.W.	5		2

TOP and CENTER: Pere Marquette No. 16691 is a good example of a 70-ton 53'6" AAR design flat car from series 16500-16749. The built date says January 1943, but the diagram sheet indicates these cars were built in July 1942. Regardless, these were probably *War Emergency* cars with steel-conserving hardwood stringers. The following 16750-16849 series was built in August-September 1944, about the time all-steel cars were allowed back into production, and would have had steel Z-bar stringers. Although some roads opted for double stringers on each side of the center sill, the AAR designs called for triple stringers. It's unknown which version the PM cars got. The 70-ton AAR design featured four main crossbearers (evident in the side view), 14 stake pockets, and a deck that was flush with the top of the bolsters and draft gear housings.

RIGHT: A Canadian National narrow-gauge G8 locomotive, built in 1956 by General Motors in London, Ontario, rides toward Newfoundland on Pere Marquette No. 16825, one of 100 flat cars built for the PM in 1944.

Built by Bethlehem Steel Company in 1941, these 70-ton gondolas were similar to series 18400-18649 built eleven years earlier (see Page 52). Like the 16500-series flat cars, this series was split between different parts suppliers. Half of the cars, Nos. 18650-18749, had Westinghouse air brakes and Miner draft gear, while the remaining cars, Nos. 18750-18849, had New York air brakes and National draft gear. These cars were not modified to any extent, but some were equipped with racks for auto frame service in the 1950s.

LEFT: Like the PM's 18400-series gondolas, these 18650-series cars were equipped with drop ends. The cars got Apex metal brake steps, with an Equipco pump-handle hand brake mounted to the B-end corner post. Note that on these "reversed" type Dreadnaught ends, the main ribs as well as the secondary "darts" all face inward.

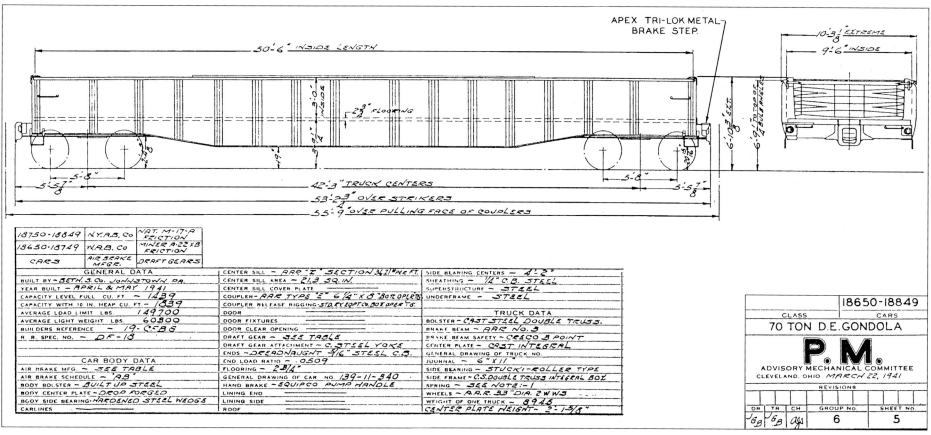

CARS	AIR BRAKE MFG.	DRAFT GEARS
18750-18849	N.Y.A.B. Co	NAT. M-17-A FRICTION
18650-18749	W.A.B. Co	MINER A-23 XB FRICTION

GENERAL DATA		
BUILT BY - BETH. S. Co. JOHNSTOWN PA.		
YEAR BUILT - APRIL & MAY 1941		
CAPACITY LEVEL FULL CU. FT. ~ 1439		
CAPACITY WITH 10 IN. HEAP CU. FT. ~ 1839		
AVERAGE LOAD LIMIT LBS. 149700		
AVERAGE LIGHT WEIGHT LBS. 60300		
BUILDERS REFERENCE ~ 19-C586		
R. R. SPEC. NO. ~ DF-13		

CAR BODY DATA
AIR BRAKE MFG. ~ SEE TABLE
AIR BRAKE SCHEDULE ~ AB
BODY BOLSTER - BUILT UP STEEL
BODY CENTER PLATE - DROP FORGED
BODY SIDE BEARING - HARDENED STEEL WEDGS
CARLINES

CENTER SILL - AAR "I" SECTION 36.2# PER FT.
CENTER SILL AREA - 21.3 SQ.IN.
CENTER SILL COVER PLATE
COUPLER - AAR, TYPE "E" 6 1/4" X 8" BOT. OPER'D
COUPLER RELEASE RIGGING - STD. EXCEPT Cs. BOT. OPER'TG.
DOOR
DOOR FIXTURES
DOOR CLEAR OPENING
DRAFT GEAR - SEE TABLE
DRAFT GEAR ATTACHMENT - C. STEEL YOKE
ENDS - DREADNAUGHT 5/16" STEEL C.B.
END LOAD RATIO ~ .0509
FLOORING ~ 2 3/4"
GENERAL DRAWING OF CAR NO. 139-11-340
HAND BRAKE - EQUIPCO PUMP HANDLE
LINING END
LINING SIDE
ROOF

SIDE BEARING CENTERS - 4'-2"
SHEATHING - 1/4" C.B. STEEL
SUPERSTRUCTURE - STEEL
UNDERFRAME - STEEL

TRUCK DATA
BOLSTER - CAST STEEL DOUBLE TRUSS.
BRAKE BEAM - AAR No. 3
BRAKE BEAM SAFETY - CELCO 3 POINT
CENTER PLATE - CAST INTEGRAL
GENERAL DRAWING OF TRUCK NO.
JOURNAL ~ 6" X 11"
SIDE BEARING - STUCKI-ROLLER TYPE
SIDE FRAME - C.S. DOUBLE TRUSS INTEGRAL BOX
SPRING ~ SEE NOTE :- 1
WHEELS ~ A.A.R. 33" DIA. 2 W.W.S
WEIGHT OF ONE TRUCK ~ 8945
CENTER PLATE HEIGHT - 3'-1-5/8"

	18650-18849
CLASS	CARS
70 TON D.E. GONDOLA	

P.M.
ADVISORY MECHANICAL COMMITTEE
CLEVELAND, OHIO MARCH 22, 1941

REVISIONS							
DR	TR	CH	GROUP NO.	SHEET NO.			
J.B.	J.B.	a.w.	6	5			

ABOVE and RIGHT: Pere Marquette 50-foot gondola No. 18686 was built in April 1941, part of an order for 200 cars delivered by Bethlehem Steel. Note the gusseted angle braces protruding from the second panel from each end. Perhaps these were for a future installation of auto frame racks. Indeed, by early 1950, 32 cars were equipped with racks for loading automobile frames. By 1961, that number had increased to 103, but now they were assigned to C&O series 218650-218849. Another 86 cars were in general service under C&O road numbers with 11 cars remaining in the original PM series, three of which had drop bottom containers for magnesite loading. In 1970, there were still 102 cars on the C&O roster with just one PM car still in service. Many of these cars were equipped for loading coil steel, wallboard or glass. Others got specialized containers for various types of minerals.

ABOVE: An in-service view of PM 70-ton gondola No. 18737 with a reweigh stencil of WY 12-48. The cars in PM series 18650-18849 had 14-side posts as opposed to the 12-posts on PM Nos. 18400-18649 built in 1930.

GSC Photo - C&OHS Collection

The Pere Marquette's last order for 70-ton gondolas came from Greenville Steel Car Company in 1944. They differed from previous orders by being two-feet longer inside. Otherwise they were quite similar. All had Westinghouse air brakes, Miner draft gear, and Dreadnaught drop ends. None were ever modified.

LEFT: Builder's photo of PM gondola No. 18948. This series of 100 cars was built in July and August 1944. By this time, the War Production Board had allowed the construction of all-steel railroad cars to resume.

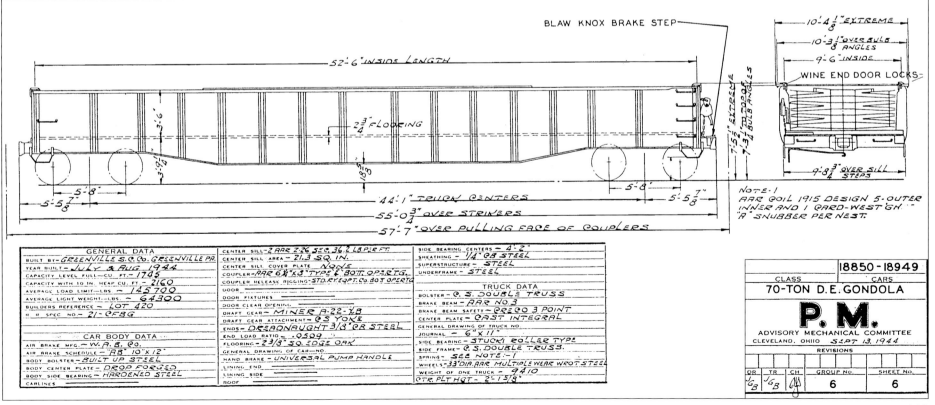

GENERAL DATA

BUILT BY -	GREENVILLE S.C. Co. GREENVILLE PA.
YEAR BUILT -	JULY & AUG. 1944
CAPACITY LEVEL FULL—CU. FT.-	1705
CAPACITY WITH 10 IN. HEAP CU. FT.-	2160
AVERAGE LOAD LIMIT—LBS. -	145700
AVERAGE LIGHT WEIGHT—LBS. -	64300
BUILDERS REFERENCE -	LOT 420
R. R. SPEC NO. -	21-QFBG

CAR BODY DATA

AIR BRAKE MFG. -	W. A. B. Co.
AIR BRAKE SCHEDULE -	"AB" 10"X12"
BODY BOLSTER -	BUILT UP STEEL
BODY CENTER PLATE -	DROP FORGED
BODY SIDE BEARING -	HARDENED STEEL
CARLINES	

CENTER SILL-	2 AAR Z-26 SEC. 36.2 LB. PER FT.
CENTER SILL AREA -	21.3 SQ. IN.
CENTER SILL COVER PLATE -	NONE
COUPLER-	AAR 6¼"X8" TYPE E BOT. OP. & TG.
COUPLER RELEASE RIGGING-	STD. RY. EQPT. Co. BOT. OPER'TG
DOOR -	
DOOR FIXTURES -	
DOOR CLEAR OPENING -	
DRAFT GEAR -	MINER A-22-18
DRAFT GEAR ATTACHMENT -	Q S YOKE
ENDS -	DREADNAUGHT 3/8 QR STEEL
END LOAD RATIO -	.0509
FLOORING -	23/8" SQ. EDGE OAK
GENERAL DRAWING OF CAR—NO. -	
HAND BRAKE -	UNIVERSAL PUMP HANDLE
LINING END -	
LINING SIDE -	
ROOF -	

SIDE BEARING CENTERS -	4'-2"
SHEATHING -	1/4" QB STEEL
SUPERSTRUCTURE -	STEEL
UNDERFRAME -	STEEL

TRUCK DATA

BOLSTER -	Q. S. DOUBLE TRUSS
BRAKE BEAM -	AAR NO 3
BRAKE BEAM SAFETY -	PRESCO 3 POINT
CENTER PLATE -	CAST INTEGRAL
GENERAL DRAWING OF TRUCK NO. -	
JOURNAL -	6"X11"
SIDE BEARING -	STUCKI ROLLER TYPE
SIDE FRAME -	Q. S. DOUBLE TRUSS
SPRING -	SEE NOTE:-1
WHEELS-33"DIA. AAR MULTIPLE WEAR WROT STEEL	
WEIGHT OF ONE TRUCK -	9410
CTR. PLT. HGT. -	2'-15/8"

18850 - 18949	
CLASS	CARS
70-TON D. E. GONDOLA	

P.M.

ADVISORY MECHANICAL COMMITTEE
CLEVELAND. OHIO   SEPT. 13. 1944

REVISIONS

DR	TR	CH	GROUP NO.	SHEET NO.
JGB	JGB		6	6

RIGHT: The ends of PM gondolas in series 18850-18949 show slight variations from the previous order of 70-ton gondolas built in 1941 (see Page 111). Both groups had Dreadnaught drop ends, but these cars received Universal pump handle hand brakes and Blaw-Knox brake steps.

BELOW: Pere Marquette 70-ton gondola No. 18948 was built in August 1944 by Greenville Steel. Like many of their 50-foot cousins, 24 of these 52'6" cars had been equipped in the mid-1950s for transporting auto frames. By 1970, there were still 16 cars in original PM road numbers, with another 66 cars assigned to C&O series 218850-218949, some of which were equipped for steel loading or shipping plate and rolled glass. General Arrangement plans for these cars were published in the *1949 Car Builders' Cyclopedia* on Page 170. A number of major roads purchased or built nearly identical gondolas circa 1940-1957, many with steel floors.

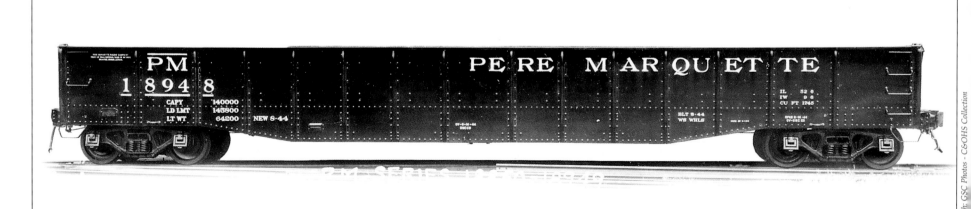

This is another box car series with a gap in it (the missing numbers are filled in by the diagram on Page 119). The cars represented here are all very similar, differing only in the brake and draft gear variations. Car Nos. 83500-83649 were built by the General American Transportation Corporation of Chicago. They have New York air brakes and National draft gear. The second order was built by AC&F, with car Nos. 83800-83899 also having New York air brakes, but Miner draft gear. Cars 83900-83999 got Westinghouse air brakes and National draft gear. All cars were equipped with Youngstown steel doors.

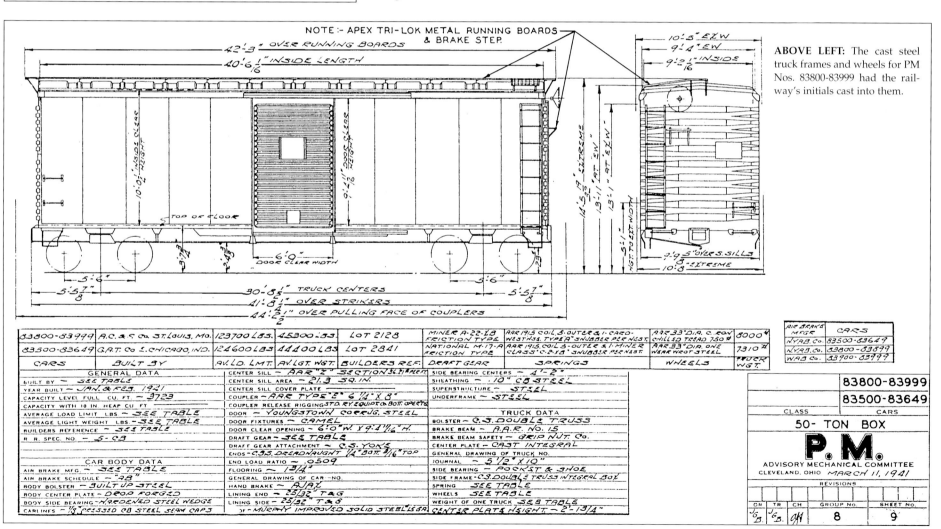

ABOVE LEFT: The cast steel truck frames and wheels for PM Nos. 83800-83999 had the railway's initials cast into them.

CARS	BUILT BY	AV. LD. LMT.	AV. LGT. WGT.	BUILDERS REF.	DRAFT GEAR	SPRINGS	WHEELS	TRUCK WGT.
83800-83999	A.C.& F. Co. ST. LOUIS, MO.	123700 LBS.	45300 LBS.	LOT 2128	MINER A-22-LB FRICTION TYPE	AAR 1915 COIL 5 OUTER & 1 CARD WSTHS. TYPE "A" SNUBBER PER NEST.	AAR 33" DIA. C. ROW CHILL SD. TREAD 750#	8000#
83500-83649	G.A.T. Co. S. CHICAGO, IND.	124600 LBS.	44100 LBS.	LOT 2841	NATIONAL M-17-A AAR 1915 COIL 5 OUTER & 1 MINER FRICTION TYPE CLASS "C-2-18" SNUBBER PER NEST.		AAR 33" DIA. ONE WEAR WROT STEEL	7310#

AIR BRAKE MFG	CARS
N.Y.A.B. Co.	83500-83649
N.Y.A.B. Co.	83800-83899
W.A.B. Co.	83900-83999

GENERAL DATA

BUILT BY — SEE TABLE	
YEAR BUILT — JAN. & FEB. 1921	
CAPACITY LEVEL FULL CU. FT. — 3723	
CAPACITY WITH 10 IN. HEAP CU. FT	
AVERAGE LOAD LIMIT LBS. — SEE TABLE	
AVERAGE LIGHT WEIGHT LBS. — SEE TABLE	
BUILDERS REFENENCE — SEE TABLE	
R. R. SPEC. NO. — 5-CB	

CENTER SILL — AAR "Z" SECTION 36.7# PER FT.	
CENTER SILL AREA — 21.3 SQ. IN.	
CENTER SILL COVER PLATE	
COUPLER — AAR TYPE "E" 6 1/4" X 8"	
COUPLER RELEASE RIGGING STD. RY EQUIP. Co. BOTT. OPER'N	
DOOR — YOUNGSTOWN CORRUG. STEEL	
DOOR FIXTURES — CAMEL	
DOOR CLEAR OPENING — 6'-0" W. X 9'-2 11/16" H.	
DRAFT GEAR — SEE TABLE	
DRAFT GEAR ATTACHMENT — C.S. YOKE	
ENDS — C.S. DREADNAUGHT 1/4" BOTT. 3/16" TOP	
END LOAD RATIO — .0509	
FLOORING — 13/4"	
GENERAL DRAWING OF CAR—NO.	
HAND BRAKE — AJAX	
LINING END — 25/32" T&G	
LINING SIDE — 25/32" T&G	
ROOF — MURPHY IMPROVED SOLID STEEL "I.S.B.A.	

SIDE BEARING CENTERS — 4'-8"	
SHEATHING — .10" CB STEEL	
SUPERSTRUCTURE — STEEL	
UNDERFRAME — STEEL	

TRUCK DATA

BOLSTER — C.S. DOUBLE TRUSS	
BRAKE BEAM — A.A.R. NO. 15	
BRAKE BEAM SAFETY — GRIP NUT. Co.	
CENTER PLATE — CAST INTEGRAL	
GENERAL DRAWING OF TRUCK NO.	
JOURNAL — 5 1/2" X 10"	
SIDE BEARING — POCK'ST & SHOE	
SIDE FRAME — C.S. DOUBLE TRUSS INTEGRAL BOX	
SPRING — SEE TABLE	
WHEELS — SEE TABLE	
WEIGHT OF ONE TRUCK — SEE TABLE	
CENTER PLATE HEIGHT — 2'-13/4"	

CAR BODY DATA

AIR BRAKE MFG. — SEE TABLE	
AIR BRAKE SCHEDULE — "AB"	
BODY BOLSTER — BUILT UP STEEL	
BODY CENTER PLATE — DROP FORGED	
BODY SIDE BEARING — HARDENED STEEL WEDGE	
CARLINES — 1/8" PRESSED CB STEEL SEAM CAPS	

83800-83999	
83500-83649	

CLASS	CARS
50-TON BOX	

P. M.

ADVISORY MECHANICAL COMMITTEE
CLEVELAND. OHIO   MARCH 11, 1941

REVISIONS

DR	TR	CH	GROUP No.	SHEET No.
J.G.B.	J.E.B.	O.H.	8	9

RIGHT: PM box car No. 83848 was built by AC&F in January 1941, part of an order for two hundred AAR 1937-design box cars in series 83800-83999. There was relatively little difference between the cars from the two builders. Note the black underframe and ends.

OPPOSITE: The interior of PM No. 83848, when new, was clean enough for handling grain. The lines near the door indicate the maximum fill levels for (bottom to top) wheat, corn and rye, and barley. These cars had single Z-section stringers on each side of the center sill. Note the bolt heads in the 1-3/4" thick wood flooring.

RIGHT: PM No. 83552 is typical of the 150 GATC-built box cars from series 83500-83649. Note that the ends on both of these cars are painted with black car cement, but while the black stops at the corners of the AC&F car, it wraps around and covers the rivet strip on this car.

ABOVE, LEFT and RIGHT: The 4/5 Dreadnaught ends of the AC&F-built box cars represent those applied to all 500 of the PM's AAR 1937-design box cars built in 1941 by General American, Pullman-Standard, and American Car & Foundry. All received Ajax power hand brakes, and Apex metal running boards and brake steps.

Radio AC&F Photos MLM Collection

PERE MARQUETTE

Pullman-Standard built 150 AAR 1937-design box cars for the Pere Marquette at the same time as the previous series with whose numbers they mesh. The only noticable difference between the three groups is the application of the Chicago Railway Equipment Company (Creco) seven-panel steel doors on the Pullman cars. Shortly thereafter, the more familiar *Superior* trade name was applied to this type of welded steel panel door.

LEFT: PM box car No. 83690 was built in January 1941 by Pullman-Standard. Like the AC&F and GATC cars, the underframes and ends were painted black. This car also has black trucks.

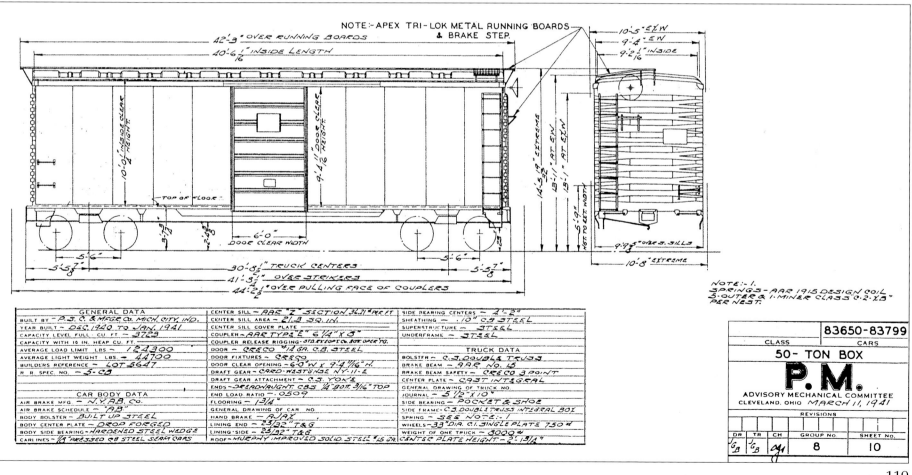

NOTE:- APEX TRI-LOK METAL RUNNING BOARDS & BRAKE STEP.

GENERAL DATA			
BUILT BY - P.S.C. & MFG. CO. MICH. CITY, IND.	CENTER SILL - AAR "Z" SECTION 36.21 # PER FT	SIDE BEARING CENTERS - 4'-2"	
YEAR BUILT ~ DEC. 1940 TO JAN. 1941	CENTER SILL AREA - 21.3 SQ. IN.	SHEATHING - .10" CB STEEL	
CAPACITY LEVEL FULL - CU. FT. ~ 3723	CENTER SILL COVER PLATE	SUPERSTRUCTURE - STEEL	
CAPACITY WITH 10 IN. HEAP CU. FT.	COUPLER ~ AAR TYPE "E" 6 1/4" X 8"	UNDERFRAME - STEEL	
AVERAGE LOAD LIMIT LBS - 124300	COUPLER RELEASE RIGGING - STD. EXCEPT CO. BOT. OPER. FIG.	TRUCK DATA	
AVERAGE LIGHT WEIGHT LBS ~ 44700	DOOR ~ CRECO #14 GA. C.B. STEEL	BOLSTER - C.S. DOUBLE TRUSS	
BUILDERS REFERENCE ~ LOT 5647	DOOR FIXTURES - CRECO	BRAKE BEAM - AAR NO. 15	
R.R. SPEC. NO. - 5-CB	DOOR CLEAR OPENING - 6'-0"W X 9'-4 11/16" H	BRAKE BEAM SAFETY - CRECO 3 POINT	
	DRAFT GEAR - CARD-WESTINGHOUSE NY-11-L	CENTER PLATE - CAST INTEGRAL	
	DRAFT GEAR ATTACHMENT - C.S. YOKE	GENERAL DRAWING OF TRUCK NO.	
	ENDS ~ DREADNAUGHT. CBS 1/4" BOTT. 3/16" TOP	JOURNAL - 5 1/2" X 10"	
CAR BODY DATA	END LOAD RATIO ~ .0509	SIDE BEARING - POCKET & SHOE	
AIR BRAKE MFG. - N.Y. A.B. CO.	FLOORING - 1 3/4"	SIDE FRAME - C.S. DOUBLE TRUSS INTEGRAL BOX	
AIR BRAKE SCHEDULE - "AB"	GENERAL DRAWING OF CAR NO.	SPRING - SEE NOTE:-1	
BODY BOLSTER - BUILT UP STEEL	HAND BRAKE - AJAX	WHEELS - 33" DIA. C.I. SINGLE PLATE 750 #	
BODY CENTER PLATE - DROP FORGED	LINING END - 23/32" T&G	WEIGHT OF ONE TRUCK - 8000 #	
BODY SIDE BEARING - HARDENED STEEL WEDGE	LINING SIDE - 23/32" T&G	CENTER PLATE HEIGHT - 2'-1 9/16"	
CARLINES - 1/8 PRESSED CB STEEL SEAM CARS	ROOF - MURPHY IMPROVED SOLID STEEL #18 GA.		

NOTE:-1. SPRINGS - AAR 1915 DESIGN COIL 5-OUTER & 1-INNER CLASS C-2-13 PER NEST.

83650-83799	
CLASS	CARS
50-TON BOX	

P.M.

ADVISORY MECHANICAL COMMITTEE
CLEVELAND, OHIO MARCH 11, 1941

REVISIONS					
DR	TR	CH	GROUP NO.		SHEET NO.
J.G.B	J.G.B	04	8		10

Although this appears to be just another series of 40-foot box cars, these cars are actually quite different from all other Pere Marquette series. The 100 cars from the 84000 series, built by Pullman-Standard, were of welded construction and light weight steel. They are three tons lighter than otherwise similar cars. Note the narrow side panels and the welded radial roof on the cars.

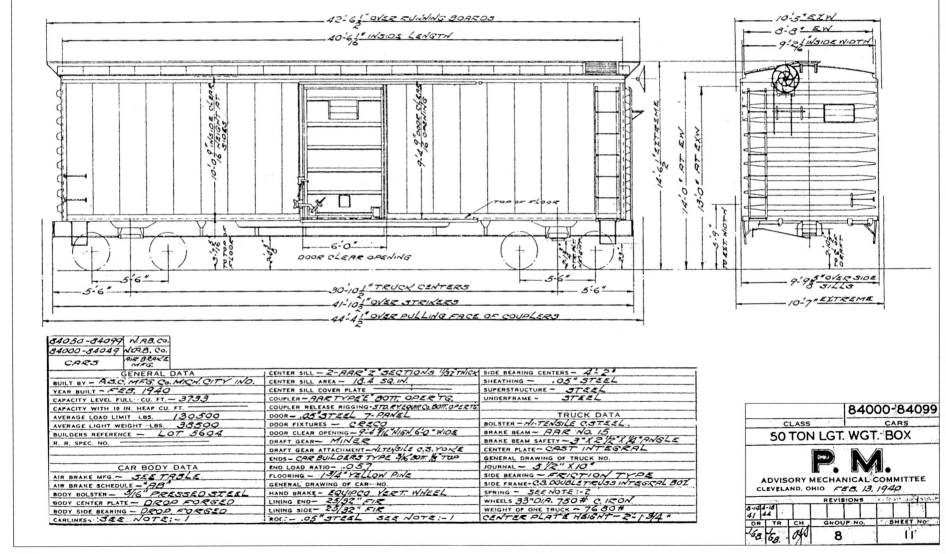

NOTE:-1
ROOF SHEETS .05" THICK, SPOT WELDED TOGETHER. CARLINES ARE AN INTEGRAL PART OF THE ROOF SHEETS AND ARE REINFORCED BY SPOT WELDING ON .05" ANGLES.
NOTE:-2
4 AAR 1936 DOUBLE COIL & 1 CARDWELL TYPE "A" SNUBBER PER NEST.

84000-84099

CLASS	CARS

50 TON LGT. WGT. BOX

P.M.
ADVISORY MECHANICAL COMMITTEE
CLEVELAND, OHIO FEB. 13, 1940

ABOVE: Pere Marquette No. 84000 outside Pullman's Haskell-Barker plant, ready for delivery in January 1940. This series was equipped with Creco seven-panel doors, Equipco hand brakes, and wood running boards. These cars were described in the trade publications of the day as a "double-sheathed light-weight 50-ton steel box car of low-alloy high-tensile steel." Identical cars were built for the Nickel Plate, Wheeling & Lake Erie, Chicago Great Western, Bessemer & Lake Erie, and Union Pacific. Note the whitewash applied to the underframe for better visibility on the publicity photo.

PERE MARQUETTE

84100 - 84399

PERE
MARQUETTE
PM
84207

ABOVE: This in-service photo of PM No. 84207 represents the cars built by GATC from series 84200-84299. These cars received US Gypsum metal running boards and brake steps.

The 300 cars of this series represented the last 40-foot box cars purchased by the Pere Marquette. These AAR 1937-design box cars were nearly identical to the cars in the 83500-83999 series. The order was split evenly into 100-car lots, each from a different builder, and therefore varying slightly as to details. Car Nos. 84100-84199 came from AC&F and had Westinghouse air brakes and National draft gear. Car Nos. 84200-84299 were built by General American with Westinghouse air brakes and Miner draft gear. The final 100 cars came from Pullman-Standard, with New York air brakes and Westinghouse draft gear. All cars had Youngstown steel doors and Ajax power hand brakes.

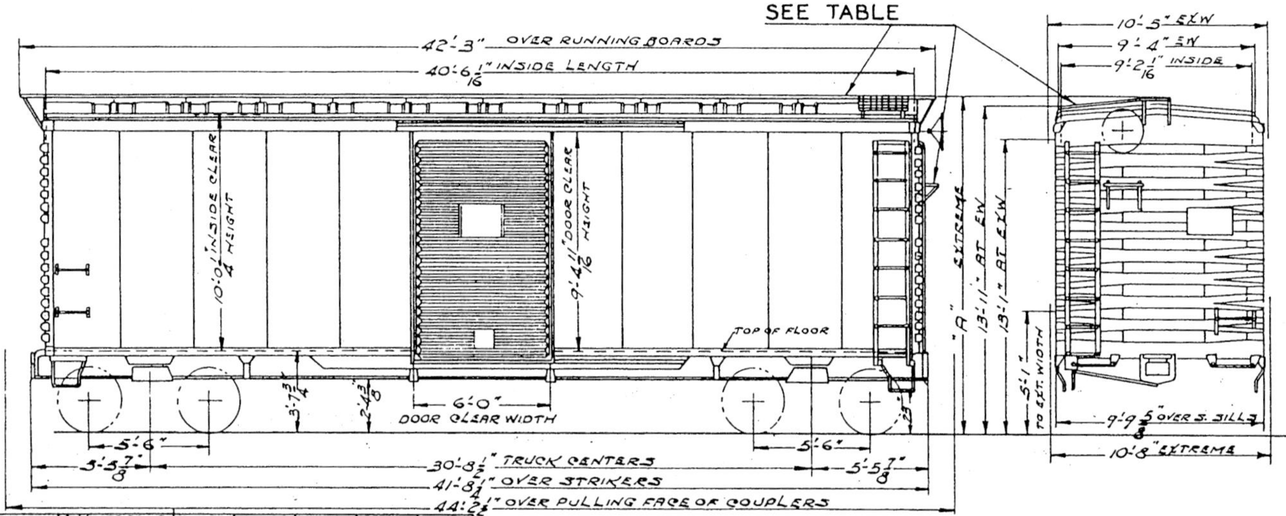
SEE TABLE
42'-3" OVER RUNNING BOARDS
40'-6 1/16" INSIDE LENGTH
10'-0 1/4" INSIDE CLEAR HEIGHT
9'-4 11/16" DOOR CLEAR HEIGHT
TOP OF FLOOR
6'-0" DOOR CLEAR WIDTH
5'-6"
5'-5 7/8"
30'-8 1/2" TRUCK CENTERS
41'-8 1/4" OVER STRIKERS
44'-2 1/2" OVER PULLING FACE OF COUPLERS
"A" EXTREME
13'-11" AT EW
13'-1" AT EXW
5'-1" TO EXT. WIDTH
10'-5" EXW
9'-4" EW
9'-2 1/16" INSIDE
9'-9 5/8" OVER SILLS
10'-8" EXTREME

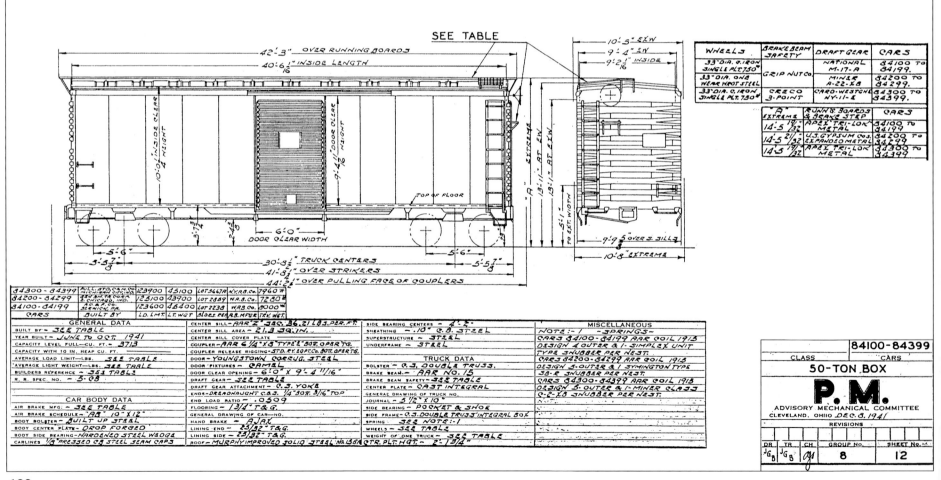

WHEELS	BRAKE BEAM SAFETY	DRAFT GEAR	CARS
33" DIA. C. IRON SINGLE PLT. 750#	GRIP NUT Co.	NATIONAL M-17-A	84100 TO 84199.
33" DIA. ONE WEAR WROT STEEL		MINER A-22-XB	84200 TO 84299.
33" DIA. C. IRON SINGLE PLT. 750#	CRECO 3-POINT	CARD-WESTGHE NY-11-E	84300 TO 84399.

"A" EXTREME	RUNN'G. BOARDS & BRAKE STEP	CARS
14'-5 19/32"	APEX "TRI-LOK" METAL	84100 TO 84199
14'-5 21/32"	U.S. GYPSUM Co's. EXPANDO METAL	84200 TO 84299
14'-5 19/32"	APEX TRI-LOK METAL	84300 TO 84399

CARS	BUILT BY	LD. LMT.	LT. WGT	BLDRS. REF.	A.B. MFGR	TRK. WGT.
84300 - 84399	PULL. STD. C. & M. Co. MICHIGAN CITY, IND.	123900	45100	LOT 5667A	N.Y.A.B. Co.	7960 #
84200 - 84299	GEN. AM. TR. CORP. E. CHICAGO, IND.	125100	43900	LOT 2889	W.A.B. Co.	7280 #
84100 - 84199	A.C. & F. Co. BERWICK, PA.	123600	46400	LOT 2238	W.A.B. Co.	8000 #

GENERAL DATA

BUILT BY - SEE TABLE
YEAR BUILT - JUNE TO OCT. 1941
CAPACITY LEVEL FULL—CU. FT. - 3713
CAPACITY WITH 10 IN. HEAP CU. FT. ——
AVERAGE LOAD LIMIT—LBS. SEE TABLE
AVERAGE LIGHT WEIGHT—LBS. SEE TABLE
BUILDERS REFERENCE - SEE TABLE
R. R. SPEC. NO. - 5-CB

CAR BODY DATA

AIR BRAKE MFG. - SEE TABLE
AIR BRAKE SCHEDULE - "AB" 10" X 12"
BODY BOLSTER - BUILT UP STEEL
BODY CENTER PLATE - DROP FORGED
BODY SIDE BEARING - HARDENED STEEL WEDGE
CARLINES 1/8" PRESSED CB STEEL SEAM CAPS

CENTER SILL - AAR "Z" SEC. 36.21 LBS. PER. FT.
CENTER SILL AREA - 21.3 SQ. IN.
CENTER SILL COVER PLATE ——
COUPLER - AAR 6 1/4" X 8" TYPE "E" BOT. OPER'TG.
COUPLER RELEASE RIGGING - STD. RY. EQPT. Co. BOTT. OPER'TG.
DOOR - YOUNGSTOWN CORRUG. STEEL
DOOR FIXTURES - CAMEL
DOOR CLEAR OPENING - 6'-0" X 9'-4 11/16"
DRAFT GEAR - SEE TABLE
DRAFT GEAR ATTACHMENT - C.S. YOKE
ENDS - DREADNAUGHT C.B.S. 1/4" BOT. 3/16" TOP
END LOAD RATIO - .0509
FLOORING - 1 3/4" T&G.
GENERAL DRAWING OF CAR—NO.
HAND BRAKE - AJAX
LINING END - 23/32" T&G.
LINING SIDE - 23/32" T&G.
ROOF - MURPHY IMPROVED SOLID STEEL No. 136A

SIDE BEARING CENTERS - 4'-2"
SHEATHING - .10" C.B. STEEL
SUPERSTRUCTURE - STEEL
UNDERFRAME - STEEL

TRUCK DATA

BOLSTER - C.S. DOUBLE TRUSS.
BRAKE BEAM - AAR NO. 15
BRAKE BEAM SAFETY - SEE TABLE
CENTER PLATE - CAST INTEGRAL
GENERAL DRAWING OF TRUCK NO.
JOURNAL - 5 1/2" X 10"
SIDE BEARING - POCKET & SHOE
SIDE FRAME - C.S. DOUBLE TRUSS INTEGRAL BOX
SPRING SEE NOTE:-1
WHEELS - SEE TABLE
WEIGHT OF ONE TRUCK - SEE TABLE
CTR. PLT. HGT. - 2'-1 3/4"

MISCELLANEOUS

NOTE:-1 -SPRINGS-
CARS 84100-84199 AAR COIL 1915 DESIGN 4 OUTER & 1-SIMPLEX UNIT TYPE SNUBBER PER NEST.
CARS 84200-84299 AAR COIL 1915 DESIGN 5-OUTER & 1 SYMINGTON TYPE SB-R SNUBBER PER NEST.
CARS 84300-84399 AAR COIL 1915 DESIGN 5-OUTER & 1-MINER CLASS C-2-XB SNUBBER PER NEST.

CLASS	84100-84399 CARS
50-TON BOX	

P. M.

ADVISORY MECHANICAL COMMITTEE
CLEVELAND, OHIO DEC. 8, 1941

REVISIONS

DR	TR	CH	GROUP No.	SHEET No.
JGB	JGB	GH	8	12

PM 84171

PM 84171

BARLEY

CORN RYE

WHEAT

AC&F Photo - C&OHS Collection

OPPOSITE: All of the Pere Marquette's AAR 1937-design box cars had single stringers, but the cars in series 84100-84399 received double stringers in the door area for additional strength. The bolt pattern is evident in this interior view of AC&F box car No. 84171.

ABOVE, LEFT and RIGHT: The AAR 1937-design featured Dreadnaught ends with a four-over-five rib pattern. Originally, square corner ends were used, but an improved version with round corners and W-section corner posts was developed. The PM used the later version, but other proprietary ends could be substituted, such as the Buckeye end applied to some of the Erie's cars. All of the PM's 84100-series cars received Ajax power hand brakes.

PERE MARQUETTE

72000 - 72099

Though this entire 100-car order represented a single order to Greenville Steel Car Company in 1940, they were divided by the Pere Marquette. The first 50 cars were equipped with a perforated steel interior lining, while the remaining cars had standard wood-sheathed interiors. All these cars had Duryea cushion underframes, the first PM revenue cars so equipped, and double Youngstown steel doors. They had black ends, underframes, and trucks. Beginning in late 1945, in what was possibly an experiment, some of the 72050-series wood lined cars were equipped for special loading of automobile frames. By early 1946, there were 37 cars dedicated to this service, but within six months all had been removed and assigned to auto parts shipments along with the other cars.

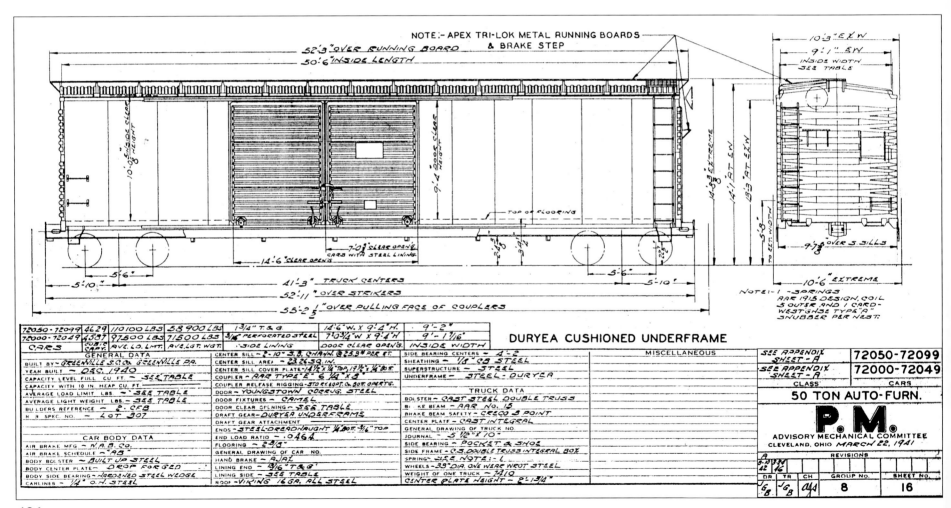

TOP: PM auto car No. 72000 represents the first of 50 cars delivered in 1940 from Greenville Steel with perforated steel interior linings for auto parts service. The auxiliary doors were rendered inoperable as the interior lining covered the entire sides of the cars, leaving only a seven-foot door opening for loading. The yellow oval on the auxiliary door is lettered *Grand Rapids*. Note the lack of the *Furniture* lettering. By 1970, the remaining 45 cars had been assigned to C&O series 272000-272049, but were listed as having a 14'6" door opening.

ABOVE: The second half of the 1940 order consisted of wood-lined cars 72050-72099. In 1961, 49 of the cars were listed under C&O series 272050-272099, 22 of which were assigned to general mechandise loading with the others in auto parts service. There were 42 cars still operating in 1970.

LEFT: Just like the PM's 40-foot box cars of the early 1940s, these auto cars received 4/5 Dreadnaught ends.

127

ABOVE: In this detail photograph of PM 72000, it is possible to see horizontal rows of rivets where the perforated steel lining is attached inside of the car. The double vertical rivet rows at the panel seams indicate U-section interior posts. All of the 72000-series cars were equipped with Ajax power hand brakes, Apex Metal running boards and brake steps, and Viking corrugated roofs, which were unpainted galvanized steel. The end was painted with black car cement as were the roof clamps. Note that the roof edge, the end of the unpainted running board, and the edge of the runnning board lateral have also been painted with overspray matching the car end. The roof edge along the car side is the same color as the car body.

Greenville Steel Car Company delivered these 50-foot auto cars in 1941. The Pere Marquette created two diagrams to cover series 72100-72199, because the first 25 cars lack end doors. That end door made the cars in series 72125-72199 four inches longer, but otherwise, the cars all appeared the same. Like the preceding series, these cars were equipped with Duryea cushion underframes, Youngstown steel doors, Viking roofs, Apex metal running boards, Apex brake steps, and Ajax power hand brakes. These cars were assigned to auto parts service for most of their existence. By 1961, all 25 cars were still in service, four of them in C&O series 272100-272124.

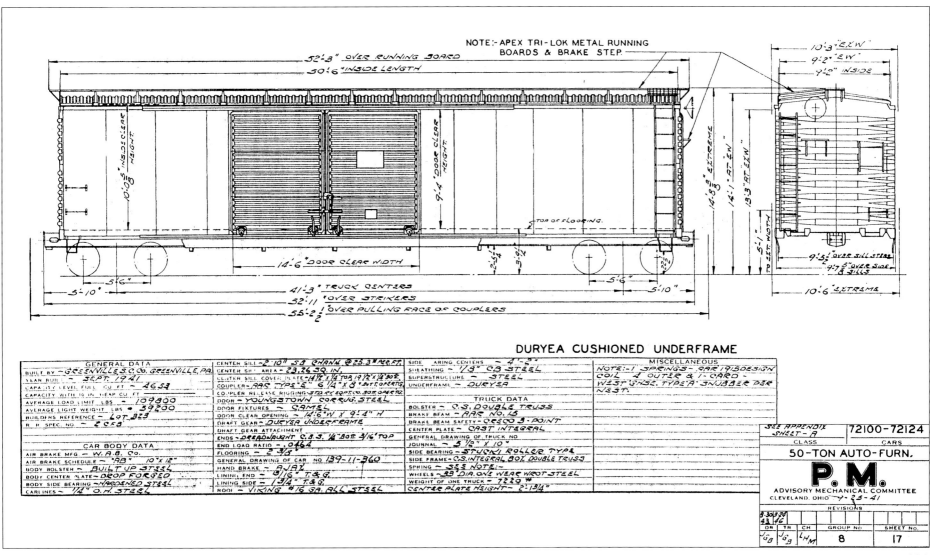

These 75 cars were equipped with Dreadnaught end loading doors, and were classified as auto parts cars for much of their service lives. By 1961, 49 of the remaining cars were renumbered into C&O series 272100-272199, with 48 of these having been relegated to general service. At the time, 24 cars were still in the original PM road numbers, with 21 of these in general service. In 1970, there were still 65 cars operating under C&O road numbers.

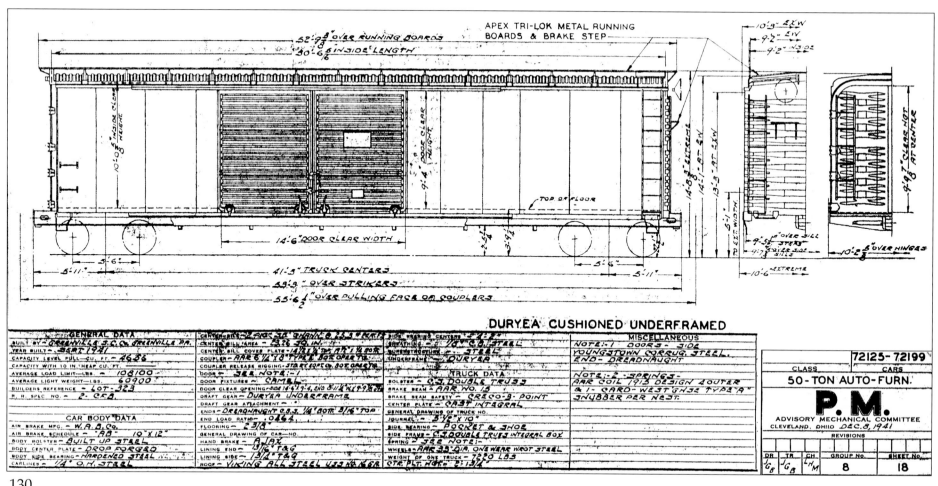

ABOVE: Pere Marquette end door equipped auto car No. 72197 was built in September 1941 by Greenville Steel. The 75 cars from series 72125-72199 were assigned to shipping auto parts for most of their careers. They had black underframes, ends, and trucks. Note that the wood interior lining was also applied to the end loading doors.

RIGHT and BELOW: PM auto car No. 72142 was also built in September 1941. Like the previous 72000-72099 series of auto cars built in 1940, all of the 72100-72199 series cars were equipped with Duryea cushion underframes. The massive Dreadnaught end doors added flexibility to the way cargo could be loaded. For example, automobile bodies could be staged more efficiently by starting at the B-end and continuing through the car body to the A-end opening, thus avoiding the need to finish loading in the center of the car when using the side doors.

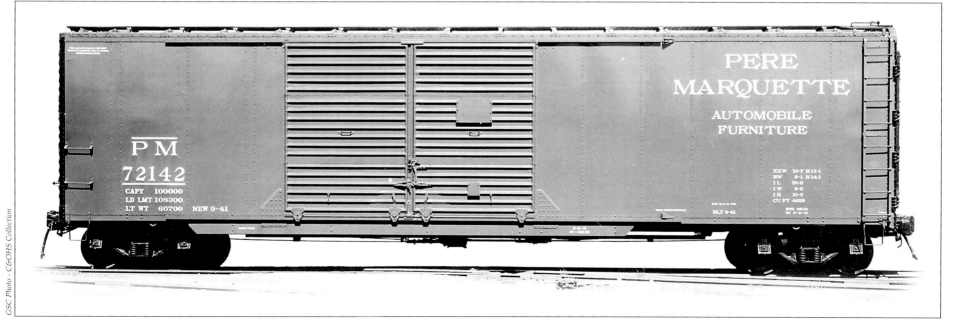

The 72200-series auto cars have the distinction of being the last cars ordered by the Pere Marquette. They were built in August through December 1946 by Ralston Steel Car Company, and arrived a scant six months before the merger into the Chesapeake & Ohio. At 15 feet, they had the largest door opening of any PM auto car. The PM again split the order; car Nos. 72200-72299 had Miner draft gear, while Nos. 72300-72399 had Waugh draft gear. All of these cars had standard, non-cushioned underframes, but car Nos. 72350-72399 did receive the perforated steel lining. Fifty cars from PM series 72200-72349 were given Evans Auto Loaders by the C&O in 1948. Car No. 72222 from this series is on display at Grand Haven, Michigan, appropriately right behind PM Berkshire No. 1223.

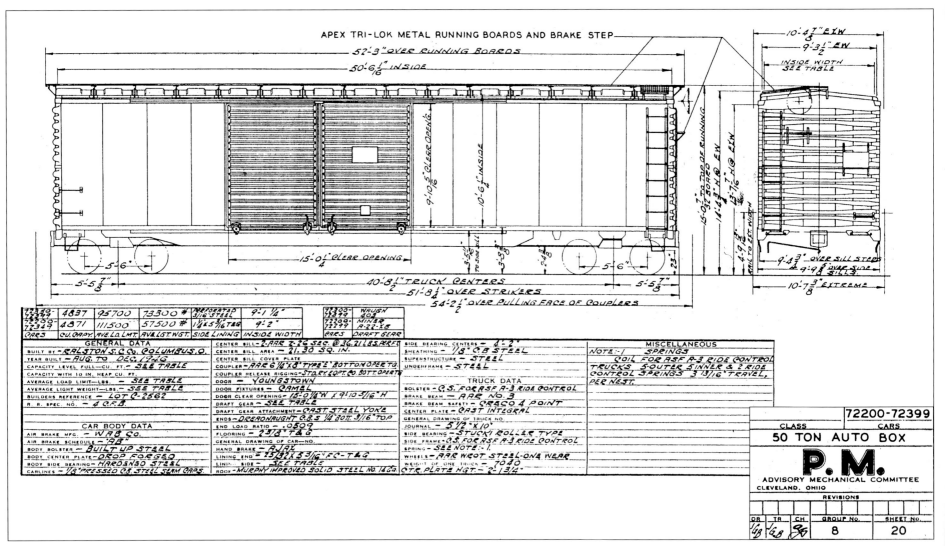

The Pere Marquette's last 50-foot auto cars were delivered with black ends, underframes, and trucks, the same scheme applied to previous orders.

ABOVE: PM No. 72367 displays the three horizontal rows of rivets used to attach the perforated steel lining to the car sides on Nos. 72350-72399. As was the case with all cars equipped with the perforated lining, the auxiliary doors were unusable. These 50 cars carried no descriptive lettering beneath the *Pere Marquette* road name on the right. All of the PM's 72200-series auto cars had four-crossbearer underframes and double stringers as in the AAR 1942-design for cars of this type. However, the railroad continued the use of U-section interior side posts in conjunction with fairly wide side panels, four to the left of the doors and six to the right (the AAR design called for Z-section posts and narrow side panels with five on the left and eight on the right). The cars were constructed with 15-foot wide door openings, which required the use of double eight-foot wide Youngstown steel doors and 15-inch channel side sill reinforcing. Perhaps more than any other PM auto cars, the 72200-series was assigned to a variety of specialized services by the C&O. In the mid-1950s, the 50 perforated steel lined cars and the 49 remaining cars with auto loaders were supplemented by 20 cars equipped with load restraining devices, an additional 65 cars in auto parts service, and 14 cars in general service. In 1961, there were still 197 cars on the roster, but 70 of these were in C&O series 272200. By 1970, almost half of the original cars were still operating, with 20 cars lasting into 1980, a true testimony of their remarkably long careers.

RIGHT: These cars also have the distinction of being the only Pere Marquette 50-foot auto cars to receive A-3 Ride Control trucks. PM covered hoppers in series 20050-20149 also used these trucks.

ABOVE: Pere Marquette auto car No. 72262 was built in September 1946 by Ralston Steel. This last series of PM auto cars had Murphy rectangular panel roofs.

LEFT: PM No. 72273 was one of the fifty cars from series 72200-72349 given auto loaders by the C&O in 1948. Note the white stripe on the main door. The "16TF" stencil indicates that this car has 16 floor tubes and Evans Type F auto loaders with 18-inch wide pans for dual-wheel trucks. The car also lacks the *Furniture* reference under the road name.

135

OPPOSITE: Typical of double-door cars on the Pere Marquette, the doors on PM series 72200-72349 were staggered to the left of center. The main doors were centered on the sides, opposite each other. The auxiliary doors are in the foreground on the right side and the background on the left side of this interior photograph of PM No. 72262.

ABOVE, LEFT and RIGHT: The Pere Marquette 50-foot auto cars built by Ralston Steel in 1946 received Standard Railway Equipment Company's *Improved* Dreadnaught ends with a four-over-four rib pattern, the only PM cars thus equipped. As with previous PM orders for 50-foot auto cars, these too had Ajax power hand brakes, and Apex metal running boards and brake steps.

PERE MARQUETTE

93400 - 93499

These were the highest numbered Pere Marquette freight cars (though not the last). They were, however, the last 40-foot auto cars built for the PM, and were similar to the 400 cars in the 93000-series that preceded them. Although the railroad had been buying 50-foot auto cars for several years, in 1941, the PM ordered an addditional 100 40-foot steel auto cars from the Ralston Steel Car Company. The PM tended to use the longer cars for auto parts and the shorter cars for shipping automobiles. Also, the PM's aging single-sheathed auto cars didn't have the extra height needed for auto loaders. The new cars were delivered without auto loaders, but Evans loaders were installed beginning in 1944. The entire series was equipped by late 1946, bringing the number of PM cars with auto racks to nearly 1,700.

ABOVE: The 40-ton double truss trucks with cast steel side frames and integral journal boxes as used under the Pere Marquette's last series of 40-foot auto cars are shown.

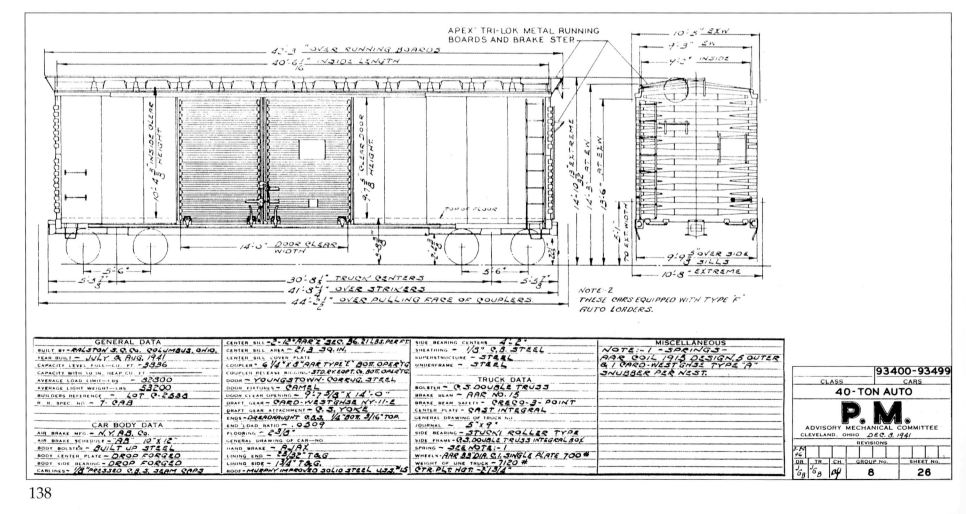

APEX TRI-LOK METAL RUNNING BOARDS AND BRAKE STEP

NOTE-2 THESE CARS EQUIPPED WITH TYPE "F" AUTO LOADERS.

GENERAL DATA				MISCELLANEOUS	
BUILT BY- RALSTON S.C. Co. COLUMBUS, OHIO.		CENTER SILL - 2-12" AAR'Z SEC. 36.21 LBS. PER FT.	SIDE BEARING CENTERS - 4-2"	NOTE:-1 -SPRINGS-	
YEAR BUILT - JULY & AUG. 1941		CENTER SILL AREA - 21.3 SQ. IN.	SHEATHING - 1/8" C.B. STEEL	AAR COIL 1913 DESIGN, 5 OUTER	
CAPACITY LEVEL FULL-CU. FT. - 3336		CENTER SILL COVER PLATE	SUPERSTRUCTURE - STEEL	& 1 CARD-WEST GH38 TYPE "A"	
CAPACITY WITH 10 IN. HEAP CU. FT		COUPLER - 6 1/4" X 8" AAR TYPE "E" BOTT. OPER'G	UNDERFRAME - STEEL	SNUBBER PER NEST.	
AVERAGE LOAD LIMIT-LBS - 82300		COUPLER RELEASE RIGGING - STD. RY. EQPT. Co. BOTT. OPER'TG			
AVERAGE LIGHT WEIGHT-LBS 53200		DOOR - YOUNGSTOWN- CORRUG. STEEL	TRUCK DATA		
BUILDERS REFERENCE - LOT C-2530		DOOR FIXTURES - CAMEL	BOLSTER - C.S. DOUBLE TRUSS		
R.R. SPEC. NO - 7-CAB		DOOR CLEAR OPENING - 9-7 5/8" X 14'-0"	BRAKE BEAM - AAR NO. 15		
		DRAFT GEAR - CARD-WEST GH38 NY-11-E	BRAKE BEAM SAFETY - CRECO-3-POINT		
CAR BODY DATA		DRAFT GEAR ATTACHMENT - C.S. YOKE	CENTER PLATE - CAST INTEGRAL	93400-93499	
AIR BRAKE MFG - N.Y. A.B. Co.		ENDS - DREADNAUGHT C.B.S. 1/4" BOTT. 3/16" TOP.	GENERAL DRAWING OF TRUCK NO.	CLASS	CARS
AIR BRAKE SCHEDULE - "AB" 10" X 12"		END LOAD RATIO - .0509	JOURNAL - 5" X 9"	40-TON AUTO	
BODY BOLSTER - BUILT UP STEEL		FLOORING - 2 3/8"	SIDE BEARING - STUCKI ROLLER TYPE	**P. M.**	
BODY CENTER PLATE - DROP FORGED		GENERAL DRAWING OF CAR-NO	SIDE FRAME - C.S. DOUBLE TRUSS INTEGRAL BOX	ADVISORY MECHANICAL COMMITTEE	
BODY SIDE BEARING - DROP FORGED		HAND BRAKE - AJAX	SPRING - SEE NOTE-1	CLEVELAND, OHIO DEC. 8, 1941	
CARLINES - 1/8 PRESSED C.B.S. SEAM CAPS		LINING END - 23/32" T&G	WHEELS - AAR 33" DIA. C.I. SINGLE PLATE 700 #	REVISIONS	
		LINING SIDE - 1 3/4" T&G.	WEIGHT OF ONE TRUCK - 7120 #		
		ROOF - MURPHY IMPROVED SOLID STEEL U.S. "15	CTR. PLT. HGT. - 2 13/4"	DR: J.G.B TR: J.G.B CH: O4 GROUP NO. 8 SHEET NO. 26	

138

There has been some controversy over the paint scheme shown on PM No. 93499. It was most probably a gray wash applied only for these builder's photographs, and removed before the car was delivered to the railroad (note that the trucks and couplers were also gray). It is highly unlikely that the car ever saw revenue service painted like this.

PM 93499

PERE
MARQUETTE

AUTOMOBILE

PM
93499
CAPY 80000
LD LMT 82900
LT WT 53100 NEW 8-41

EX W 10·5 H13·6·
E W 9·3 H14·3
I L 40·6
I W 9·2
I H 10·4
CU FT 3836

BLT 8-41   RPKD A.S.C.CO
             COL 6-12-41

ABOVE: Although No. 93499 received the publicity gray paint scheme, the galvanized steel roof was unpainted, as were the Apex running boards. Note that the seam caps and the grabiron have been coated with black car cement. This was a common practice during this era, and the roofs on the entire series were probably done this way. Like the PM's 72200-series 50-foot auto cars, these cars received Murphy rectangular panel steel roofs.

RIGHT: The Pere Marquette's last series of 40-foot auto cars received Dreadnaught ends with a five-over-five rib pattern, typical of box and auto cars built in the early and mid-1940s with increased interior height. They were the only PM cars with this type of end. The Ajax power hand brake was a PM favorite.

LEFT: Except with regard to the ends and roofs, the Pere Marquette's last order for 40-foot auto cars was built in 1941 and shared construction features with the previous 93000-93399 series delivered in 1936. Both series were built by Ralston Steel with double Youngstown steel doors over a 14-foot door opening, U-section interior side posts, and two-crossbearer underframes with single stringers. However, the 1941 cars received Murphy roofs, 5/5 Dreadnaught ends, Apex metal running boards, and seven-rung side ladders, whereas the 1936 cars had Viking roofs, recessed type Dreadnaught ends, wood running boards, and eight-rung ladders.

BELOW: Pere Marquette auto car No. 93422 was at San Francisco in April 1955. Last reweighed at the Wyoming Shops in November 1951, the car is equipped with Evans Type F auto loading racks and 12 floor tubes. Although not delivered with auto loaders, the entire series was so equipped by late 1946. Ten years later, there were still 98 cars with auto loaders. By 1961, they had been renumbered into C&O series 293400-293499, with 47 auto loader cars remaining and 47 cars assigned to general service. The last car was on the roster until 1970.

141

The car with the claim to being the last Pere Marquette freight car is this one. The one and only PM plug-door car was built in the Wyoming Shops in April 1947, only two months before the end of the Pere Marquette as an independent railroad. The car was most likely converted from an 89350-series box car and had new sides with plug doors added. The interior was insulated. Whether this car was to have been the prototype of a whole series is a question we will never be able to answer, for the C&O merger ended any such plan if there was one. No diagram for this car exists.

The interior of most Pere Marquette box and auto cars was wood. Bracing for load restraint was simply nailed in place wherever it was needed. Beginning in 1938, however, several series of PM auto cars had a remarkable perforated steel interior lining installed, which entirely covered the side walls. The top photograph shows the lining in place, marked in one-foot squares. The bottom photograph shows how crossmembers could be positioned inside and securely fastened to the metal grid. Although shown in neat arrangement for the photograph, these crossmembers could actually be placed anywhere they were needed.

Perforated Steel Lining Installations

YEAR	CAR NUMBERS
1938	PM 71250-71310
1939	PM 71317-71337
1940	PM 72000-72049 (as built)
1942	PM 71065-71075
1946	PM 72350-72399 (as built)

A number of the rebuilding, modification, and subsequent renumbering programs began by the Pere Marquette were continued after the June 6, 1947 merger with the C&O. More than 100 cars emerged from these programs still lettered for the Pere Marquette! Some series were lettered C&O from the beginning, but the C&O created their own number series for PM cars by simply placing the digit "2" in front of the PM number, thus continuing the PM tradition.

ABOVE: C&O box car No. 291644 is a former Pere Marquette auto car from series 90350-91849 (see Page 89). This June 1930 Pullman product was converted to a single-door car at the Wyoming Shops in November 1954. Originally PM auto car No. 91644, this car has been renumbered into C&O series 290350-291849. According to the November 17, 1952 issue of *Railway Age* magazine, the C&O initiated a program to rebuild 600 of these auto cars into single-door cars suitable for loading bulk commodities such as flour, grain, and sugar. Prefabricated steel panels were installed in place of the auxiliary doors, which were salvaged for use as replacement doors. Note the offset door reinforcing under the side sill, a sure spotting feature of a former auto car. By the mid-1950s, more than 1,000 of the 90350-series cars had been converted to single-door and renumbered. Almost 80 of these were assigned to auto parts service by the C&O and placed in series 254350-254375 and 260076-260127. Note that the C&O logo has simulated "smoke" coming from the word *Progress*, which was previously a steam powered train. The next version replaced the smoke with a stylized "speed" line.

Paul Dunn Photo - Richard Burg Collection

ABOVE: Former PM box car No. 282732 is still in its original condition (see Page 81), but it has been renumbered into C&O series 282000-283499. The C&O also assigned 76 of these former 82000-series cars to series 254400-254470 and 258000-258004 for auto parts service. This car was repainted at C&O's Raceland, Kentucky, shops in July 1959, after repairs to the lower car side.

BELOW: C&O box car No. 257124 is a rebuilt PM auto car from series 89350-90349 (see Page 77). Fifty of these steel rebuilds were renumbered into C&O series 257100-257149 and equipped with Evans Damage-Free loaders. Note the "DF-8" stencil on the panel to the right of the road number. This view shows the original Hutchins end and the method of attaching the new steel car sides to the side sill.

Al Kresse Collection

	Post-Merger PM Series				
	SERIES	CU FT	D.O.	FORMER SERIES	FIRST APPEARED
PM	54055-54059	3,712	6'	89350-90349	1949
PM	54200-54240	3,170	6'	85000-87499	1948
PM	54250-54254	3,712	6'	89350-90349	1949
PM	54260-54274	3,403	6'	88350-89299	1951
PM	54550	3,712	6'	89350-90349	1949
PM	54800-54835	3,712	6'	89350-90349	1950
PM	55100	3,403	6'	88350-89299	1949
PM	55600-55694+	3,712	12'	89350-90349	1949
PM	55750-55779+	3,712	12'	89350-90349	1948
PM	56200*	3,712	12'	*90350-91849	1949
PM	56300-56316	3,712	6'	89350-90349	1948
PM	65062-65069	3,712	6'	89350-90349	1949
C&O	254265	3,403	6'	88350-89299	1951
C&O	254307	3,403	6'	88350-89299	1950
C&O	254350-254375*	3,712	6'	*90350-91849	1953
C&O	254400-254470*	3,053	6'	*82000-83499	1949
C&O	254551-254593	3,712	6'	89350-90349	1949
C&O	254800-254835	3,712	6'	89350-90349	1950
C&O	254836-254845*	3,712	12'	*90350-91849	1953
C&O	254900-254924	3,712	6'	89350-90349	1950
C&O	255100	3,403	6'	88350-89299	1955
C&O	255200-255235	3,712	6'	89350-90349	1949
C&O	255600-255781*	3,712	12'	*90350-91849	1949
C&O	256200*	3,712	12'	*90350-91849	1956
C&O	256317-256329	3,712	6'	89350-90349	1948
C&O	257000-257059*	3,712	12'	*90350-91849	1948
C&O	257100-257149**	3,712	6'	89350-90349	1951
C&O	258000-258004*	3,053	6'	*82000-83499	1948
C&O	260076-260127*	3,712	6'	*90350-91849	1953

*All-steel cars   **All-steel rebuilds   +Single-sheathed cars retained use of auxiliary doors

RIGHT: C&O single-door box car No. 289698 is a former PM single-sheathed auto car built in July 1929 from series 89350-90349 (see Page 77). It has been extensively rebuilt with new steel sides, roof, and running boards, and is now equipped with the post-war type Youngstown steel doors and AB brakes. It is shown in the C&O's black paint scheme applied at their Raceland shops (RA 10-60). Over 775 of these steel rebuilds were in general service on the C&O's roster in series 289350-290349. A few were assigned to auto parts service or other specific commodity loading within the same number series. An additional 50 cars were equipped with Evans DF loaders and given Nos. 257100-257149 (see lower photo on Page 145).

Paul Dunn Photo - Richard Burg Collection

RIGHT: C&O car No. 257016 is a former PM 90350-91849 series auto car that has been renumbered and equipped with Evans DF loaders (note the *Damage Free Loader* lettering on the auxiliary door and the "DF" symbol on the main door). The car has been upgraded with AB brakes and Apex metal running boards and brake step, but is otherwise still in its original condition as built in June 1930. This car is from a group of 60 cars in C&O series 257000-257059 that received DF loaders for merchandise loading in 1948. It was reweighed at PM's Rougemere Yard in Detroit. Another 40 of these ex-PM cars were assigned to C&O auto parts service in various number series. All retained the use of their double-doors. In addition, more than 75 of these cars were in auto parts service with six-foot door openings (the auxiliary doors were probably sealed shut).

Al Kresse Collection

*All-steel cars   **All-steel rebuilds

ROAD NOS.	C.F.	O.L.	D.O.	JUL 1949	APR 1950	JAN 1952	OCT 1954	JUL 1956	JUL 1961	CLASS	FORMER SERIES
254265	3,403	42'6"	6'	–	–	1	–	–	–	XAP	88350-89299
"				–	–	–	1	–	–	XM	" "
254307	3,403	42'6"	6'	–	1	–	–	–	–	XAP	88350-89299
254350-254375*	3,712	42'3"	6'	–	–	–	26	–	–	XAP	* 90350-91849
" "					–	–	–	26	24	XM	" "
254400-254470*	3,053	42'3"	6'	–	61	71	71	59	5	XAP	* 82000-83499
" "				–	–	–	–	12	2	XM	" "
254551-254593	3,712	42'6"	6'	30	41	29	4	–	–	XAP	89350-90349
" "				–	–	1	26	–	–	XM	" "
254800-254835	3,712	42'6"	6'	–	–	10	10	5	–	XAP	89350-90349
" "				–	–	–	–	5	–	XM	" "
254836-254845*	3,712	42'3"	12'	–	–	–	10	8	–	XAP	* 90350-91849
257900-254924	3,712	42'6"	6'	–	–	24	23	23	–	XMP	89350-90349
255100	3,403	42'6"	6'	–	–	–	–	1	–	XAP	88350-89299
255210-255214	3,712	42'6"	6'	5	–	–	–	–	–	XMP	89350-90349
255200-255235	3,712	42'6"	6'	–	15	27	31	35	34	XMP	89350-90349
255600-255781*	3,712	42'3"	12'	27	27	29	28	31	–	XAP	* 90350-91849
" "	3,712	42'6"	12'	–	–	–	6	2	2	XM	89350-90349
256200*	3,712	42'3"	12'	–	–	–	–	1	1	XAP	* 90350-91849
256317-256329	3,712	42'6"	6'	8	13	–	–	–	–	XMP	89350-90349
257000-257059*	3,712	42'3"	12'	60	–	–	–	59	59	XME	* 90350-91849
" "				–	60	–	–	–	–	XM	" "
" "				–	–	59	59	–	–	XMP	" "
257100-257149**	3,712	42'6"	6'	–	–	50	50	–	–	XML	89350-90349
" "				–	–	–	–	50	50	XME	" "
258000-258004*	3,053	42'3"	6'	2	5	–	–	–	–	XAP	* 82000-83499
" "				–	–	5	5	5	2	XM	" "
260076-260127*	3,712	42'3"	6'	–	–	–	51	–	–	XAP	* 90350-91849
" "				–	–	–	–	10	–	XM	" "

In the late 1930s and 1940s, the Pere Marquette initiated various special number series for cars assigned to auto parts or other special services. Many of these assignments continued after the merger, with the Chesapeake & Ohio expanding the concept within their own numbering system for ex-PM cars (identified by the additional digit "2" in front of the number series). Usually, the Pere Marquette number series intermix with the C&O numbers without conflict. One exception is Pere Marquette series 54800-54835 (26 XAP cars). C&O number series 254800-254835 (10 XAP cars) also existed, but the combined amount of 36 cars exactly reflects the road numbers available in both series. Another example is the 255600-255781 series of steel cars. The Pere Marquette also had cars in their 55600-55779 series, but these were not steel cars. Later some of these PM cars were transferred to the C&O series, but were then listed as "exceptions." In some cases, individual cars, such as PM Nos. 55100 and 56200, were transferred to the C&O as Nos. 255100 and 256200. The

above chart, which is based on *Official Railway Equipment Register* entries, is useful for determining the original Pere Marquette car series, which ones were single-sheathed or all-steel, and if the cars had been converted to single-door or remained as-built. The door opening (D.O.) is included, as well as the Cubic Feet (C.F.) and the Outside Length (O.L.). Note that all of the steel cars have a 42'3" outside length except for series 257100-257149, which are clearly steel rebuilds from cars in series 89350-90349. Many of these auto parts cars were former 88350 and 89350-series single-sheathed cars with six-foot door openings. Some of these may have had their auxiliary doors permanently closed (see Page 75 for a former 88350-series), but most were converted to single-door cars (see Page 80 for an example of an 89350-series). Note also, that many of the 90350-series all-steel cars retained the use of their double-doors. Those that didn't (the 254350 and 260076-series), probably had their auxiliary doors sealed shut.

PERE
MARQUETTE

4 Modeling Pere Marquette Freight Cars

Modeling PM freight cars in the early days meant scratchbuilding, painting and hand-lettering cars to closely match the prototype. Commercial kits were almost non-existent. The following is a list, non-inclusive, of most of the production models produced in HO scale over the years. This list may not include car kits that were special runs during that time.

One of the earliest kits produced was a wood one with preprinted cardstock sides and ends of PM caboose No. A801. This kit was produced by the Ideal Model Co. in the 1930s.

After WWII, Globe (later Athearn), produced a stamped metal box car kit, and during the 1948/1950 era made about 15 different car numbers of PM box cars, mostly numbered in the 84000 series. Some of these models had "glow-in-the-dark" lettering on them, which the prototype never had. Later, Athearn sold that line to George Menzies and he produced one more PM box car in that line. Athearn switched over to plastic injection-molded car kits and made kit #5052, PM 50' auto car No. 72142. While this kit was close, it didn't match the prototype because that car number was for a PM end-door car with Viking roof, neither of which the car kit had.

The WISE/NMRA had MDC run their model of the 40' gondola PM No. 10200 in conjunction with the WISE Chapter selling auto frames that were carried in the prototype PM gondolas. This was a special run only and was never repeated.

Con-Cor had some wooden craftsman type box car kits of the USRA double-sheathed box car. The kits came with pre-painted sides and at least two PM models are known to exist, car Nos. 81632 and 64046.

Ulrich came out with a combination wood and die-cast car kit in the 1950s of PM outside braced box car No. 89920. The sides were pre-painted and the ends and outside bracing were die-cast.

Silver Streak (now Walthers) lists their kit #929-222, which is for PM wooden box car No. 85100.

Red Ball (later Wabash Valley) produced a wood and die-cast craftsman type kit of PM auto car No. 89399.

Bev-Bel, using the Athearn model, made a special run of PM twin hopper No. 13512. The lettering on this model shows the lettering as it appeared originally on the PM cars.

Yankee Clipper sold a cast resin box car kit for the PM 82000 series.

With the formation of the Pere Marquette Historical Society, Inc. in 1995, more PM models have appeared because it's the policy of the society to provide model manufacturers with the most accurate prototype data to produce models of PM cars. One of the first to take advantage of this service was Red Caboose. That company has made two production runs of the 40' flat car, which the PM series 16000-16099 fit right in, with eight different car numbers.

Life-Like Proto 2000 produced a 50' drop-end gondola for PM series 18850-18949, with 12 different car numbers.

Although Bowser didn't use the services of the PMHS, they have produced a model of the AC&F 70-ton covered hopper and have made three or four production runs of PM cars in the series 20000-20149. There were a dozen different car numbers in each run.

Athearn produced a five-pack of PM hoppers using their 34' ribbed side hopper car kit as a basis for the model.

Sunshine Models produced a gray urethane casting kit of the PM series 16500-16849 series 70-ton flat cars.

The PMHS itself has commissioned special run kits as fund-raisers for the society. The first models were run using the Accurail USRA 55-ton twin hopper. Two different numbers were offered, PM Nos. 13000 and 14449. Accurail has recently released PM No. 13826 as part of its regular line.

As part of the Pere Marquette Centennial Celebration in the year 2000, the PMHS had Red Caboose produce PM box car No. 84100, and as a continuing part of that celebration, is having PM box car Nos. 83551 and 83690 produced.

The PM and freight car modelers have had some choices in car kits over the years. The older models are said to be highly desirable and collectable.

Modeling Pere Marquette freight cars is very straightforward. PM auto, box cars and stock cars were painted Boxcar Red with white lettering. PM covered hoppers, flat cars, gondolas and hoppers were painted black with white lettering. The refrigerator cars that the PM built from FGE plans were painted just like FGE cars; reefer yellow with black lettering and hardware, and Boxcar Red roof and ends with white lettering.

Lettering material for PM freight cars is available in both decal and dry-transfer form. Champ makes Road Name decal set #HN-79. This set has a "thinner" decal film, but the letter "q" doesn't have the unique "stand-off" tail.

Walthers makes decal set #934-78060 for PM freight cars, and while the decal

film is thicker in this set, it does contain some different lettering styles used by the PM over the years.

For those modelers who prefer to use dry transfers, Clover House makes some sets for the older (1900 era) PM cars.

Campbell Road makes a set for PM cars in the 1930 era.

C-D-S makes dry transfers for PM 40' and 50' cars.

For those modelers who like brass models, there are a few models produced that could be used for PM cars. The Pecos River Brass covered hopper (#2606) can be used for the PM 20000 series. Overland, at one time, made USRA hopper cars. Both A. W. Enterprises and Oriental Limited Inc. produced a brass ready-to-run box car that represents what the railfan community refers to as the PS-0 box car and represents PM series 84000-84099.

With all the cross-kit and kitbashing going on and all the detail parts now available, just about any type of PM freight car can be modeled with some time, effort and funds. The Pere Marquette was very fond of using Hutchins ends on its box cars and, luckily, Westerfield Models makes that end in HO, and photos in this chapter show how John Paton used those ends to model the PM 86000 series box cars. It's not the intention of this chapter to go into detail on how to model PM freight cars, it is the purpose to make you aware of what has been and is available in the marketplace.

John Paton, as a sideline, did custom painting services under the name Clifton Forge South. As the name implies, John specialized in custom painting C&O brass models, but if the material was available, he would do plastic models and, of course, the PM! What follows are photos of some of the PM freight cars he has modeled (all photos by Paton).

RIGHT: Westerfield Hutchins end applied to a Walthers box car to create a PM 86000 series model.

LEFT: End view of Pecos River covered hopper.

The Globe/Athearn stamped-metal with pre-painted sides, HO box car kit.

Pecos River Brass #2602 covered hopper, custom painted for PM No. 20034.

Front-Range, 50' auto car with side sill modified for PM 72300-series.

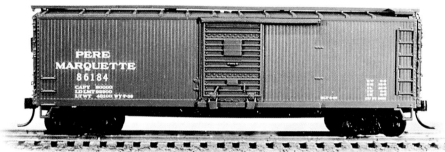

Walthers box car kit with metal door applied.
PM 86000-series with Westerfield Hutchins ends applied.

Walthers box car kit custom painted for PM 82000-series.

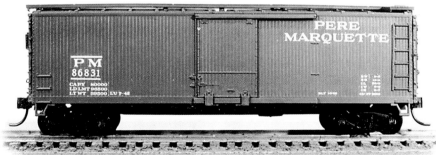

Walthers box car kit with wooden door applied.
PM 86000-series with Westerfield Hutchins ends applied.

PERE
MARQUETTE

152

Appendix A

All-Time Roster
of
Pere Marquette
Revenue Freight Cars

Compiled by
Arthur B. Million and Carl W. Shaver

SOURCES:
Pere Marquette Annual Reports, 1900-1947.
The Official Railway Equipment Register (Pere Marquette, Chesapeake & Ohio, and CSX Transportation listings, 1900-1989).
Pere Marquette Diagrams of Freight Cars, March 23, 1945 (back-dated to 1931).
Pere Marquette Railroad Company Statement of Rolling Stock, June 30, 1907.
Interstate Commerce Commission *Valuation Report* for the Pere Marquette Railway Company, 1916.
"Pere Marquette Freight Equipment," *The Chesapeake & Ohio Historical Newsletter*, August 1977 (pages 11-15).

Insulated Box and Refrigerator Cars

NUMBERS	DESCRIPTION	LL	CU.FT.	LBS.	BUILDER	DATES	RETIRED	PAGE	NOTES
1-10	Refrigerator (wood)	27'6"	---	50,000	---	1889	1921	---	---
11-110	Refrigerator (wood)	32'1"	---	60,000	Wells & French	1889	1921	---	---
111	Refrigerator (wood)	33'4"	---	60,000	Wells & French	1889	1921	---	---
25000-25299	Refrigerator (steel u.f.)	33'2"	1,880	80,000	PM (Wyoming Shops)	1924	1940	55	1
26000-26049	Produce, insulated (steel u.f.)	39'8"	2,370	80,000	PM (Wyoming Shops)	1924	---	---	2
66001-66025	Box (steel underframe)	39'7"	2,370	80,000	PM (Wyoming Shops)	1924	1953	55	3
67001-67010	Insulated Box (steel u.f.)	33'2"	1,880	80,000	PM (Wyoming Shops)	1924	1945	55	4
69001-69004	Insulated Box (steel u.f.)	39'7"	2,370	80,000	PM (Wyoming Shops)	1924	1951	55	5
69011-69018	Insulated Box (steel u.f.)	40'6"	2,896	80,000	Western Steel Car & Foundry	1922-23	1954	64	6
56200	Insulated Box (plug door)	40'6"	3,536	80,000	Pressed Steel Car Co.	1929	1972	142	7

1. 125 cars sold to Fruit Growers Express Co., 1939 (FGEX 16100-16299) 131 sold to Hyman-Michaels Co.
2. Were to be modified from PM series 25000-25299; probably never existed (appeared only in 7/37, *Official Railway Equipment Register*).
3. Rebuilt from PM series 25000-25299; equipped to handle motor hubs and drums.
4. Rebuilt from PM series 25000-25299; equipped to handle Kelsey-Hayes Company wheels.
5. Rebuilt from PM series 25000-25299; fitted for chemical service.
6. Converted in 1946, probably from PM series 85000-85999.
7. Converted in 1947, probably from PM series 89350-90349.

Stock Cars

NUMBERS	DESCRIPTION	LL	CU.FT.	LBS.	BUILDER	DATES	RETIRED	PAGE	NOTES
1900-1907	Stock, single door	39'0"	---	40,000	---	18--	1908	---	---
1908-1914	Stock, single door	32'6"	---	40,000	---	18--	1920	---	---
1915-1969	Stock, single door	33'0"	---	28-40,000	---	1890	1924	---	1
1970-1999	Stock, single door	29'0"	2,442	60,000	---	1891	1934	---	---
2000-2199 (1st)	Stock, single door	38'0"	2,362	60,000	American Car & Foundry Co.	1903	1934	12	---
2000-2049 (2nd)	Stock, single door	40'6"	3,403	80,000	Pressed Steel Car Co.	1927	1971	36	2
2200-2249	Stock, double door	38'0"	2,362	60,000	American Car & Foundry Co.	1903	1934	13	---
2250-2308	Stock, double door	38'0"	2,362	60,000	American Car & Foundry Co.	1908	1934	12	---
2400-2499	Stock, single door	36'0"	2,448	60,000	American Car & Foundry Co.	1905	1934	14	---

1. Cars with capacity of 28,000 pounds retired by 1915.
2. PM 2000-2049 (2nd) converted from box cars in PM series 89300-89349 in 1934.

Gondola and Early Coal Cars

NUMBERS	DESCRIPTION	LL	CU.FT.	LBS.	BUILDER	DATES	RETIRED	PAGE	NOTES
9001-9100	Coal, drop bottom	35'6"	---	60,000	Wells and French	1899	1929	---	---
9101-9200	Coal	34'10"	---	60,000	American Car & Foundry Co.	1899	1929	15	---
9201-9300	Coal, drop bottom	34'10"	---	60,000	American Car & Foundry Co.	1900	1929	16	---
9301-9400	Coal	34'10"	---	60,000	American Car & Foundry Co.	1901	1929	---	---
9450-9499	Coal	32'6"	---	60,000	Michigan Car Co.	18--	1921	---	---
9500-9599	Coal	35'6"	1,190	60,000	Michigan Car Co.	1891	1926	---	---
9600-9699	Coal	---	---	35-60,000	---	18--	1927	---	---
9700-9799	Coal	---	---	60,000	---	1896	1920	---	---
9800-9849	Coal	---	1,100	50,000	Haskell and Barker Car Co.	1894	1920	---	---
9850-9949	Coal	---	---	60,000	Michigan Car Co.	1891	1920	---	---
9969-9999	Coal	19'4"-31'0"	--	24-40,000	---	18--	1910	---	---
10000-10199 (1st)	Coal	35'6"	1,011	100,000	American Car & Foundry Co.	1902	1929	---	---
10000-10059 (2nd)	Gondola, steel	40'6"	1,899	100,000	Ralston Steel Car Co.	1930	1967	48	1
10060-10072 (2nd)	Gondola, steel	40'6"	1,899	100,000	Ralston Steel Car Co.	1930	1955	48	1
10100-10169 (2nd)	Gondola, steel	50'6"	1,439	140,000	Greenville Steel Car Co.	1930	1955	52	2
10170-10186 (2nd)	Gondola, steel	50'6"	1,439	140,000	Greenville Steel Car Co.	1930	1941	52	2
10200-10249	Gondola, steel	40'6"	1,899	100,000	Ralston Steel Car Co.	1930	1966	48	1
10250-10999	Gondola, wood (coal)	36'0"	1,316	80,000	American Car & Foundry Co.	1906	1934	16	---
11000-11089	Gondola, wood (coal)	32'1"	---	60,000	F. M. Hicks	1903	1930	---	---
11100-11199	Gondola, wood (coal)	36'6"	1,202	80,000	American Car & Foundry Co.	1905	1930	---	---
11200-11999	Gondola, wood (coal)	36'6"	1,202	80,000	American Car & Foundry Co.	1903	1930	17	---
12000-12799	Gondola, wood (drop-end)	35'1"	1,146	80,000	American Car & Foundry Co.	1903	1930	18	---
12800-12899	Gondola, wood (side-dump)	33'4"	953	80,000	American Car & Foundry Co.	1903	1924	19	---
12900-12999	Gondola, wood (side-dump)	36'6"	953	80,000	American Car & Foundry Co.	1905	1930	---	---
13000-13199 (1st)	Gondola, wood (side-dump)	31'6"	937	60,000	(acquired second-hand)	---	1919	---	3
17000-17249	Gondola, composite	42'0"	1,980	110,000	Illinois Car & Mfg. Co.	1927	1967	45	4
17250-17649	Gondola, composite	42'0"	1,980	110,000	Magor Car Corp.	1929	1976	46	5
17650-18399	Gondola, steel (wood floor)	40'6"	1,899	100,000	Ralston Steel Car Co.	1930	1983	48	---
18400-18649	Gondola, steel (drop-end)	50'6"	1,439	140,000	Greenville Steel Car Co.	1930	1974	52	---
18650-18849	Gondola, steel (drop-end)	50'6"	1,439	140,000	Bethlehem Steel Co.	1941	1986	111	---
18850-18949	Gondola, steel (drop-end)	52'6"	1,745	140,000	Greenville Steel Car Co.	1944	1987	113	---

1. Equipped for auto frame service; renumbered from PM series 17650-18399.
2. Equipped for auto frame service; renumbered from PM series 18400-18649.
3. Acquired approximately 1913.
4. Wooden siding replaced with steel sides, 1932-1940. Drop-bottom outlets replaced by solid floor, 1944-1953.
5. Wooden siding replaced with steel sides, 1937-1942.

Open and Covered Hopper Cars

NUMBERS	DESCRIPTION	LL	CU.FT.	LBS.	BUILDER	DATES	RETIRED	PAGE	NOTES
13000-13499 (2nd)	Hopper, USRA (steel, twin)	30'6"	1,880	110,000	Ralston Steel Car Co.	1919	1954	37	1
13500-13999 (2nd)	Hopper, USRA (steel, twin)	30'6"	1,880	110,000	American Car & Foundry Co.	1920	1955	37	1, 2
14000-14499 (2nd)	Hopper (steel, twin)	30'6"	1,880	110,000	Ralston Steel Car Co.	1923	1954	39	1
15000-15249	Hopper (steel, triple)	40'0"	2,710	140,000	Standard Steel Car Co.	1927	1957	41	3
20000-20024 (2nd)	Covered Hopper (twin)	29'3"	1,958	140,000	American Car & Foundry Co.	1942	1988	100	---
20025-20049 (2nd)	Covered Hopper (twin)	29'3"	1,958	140,000	American Car & Foundry Co.	1944	1988	104	---
20050-20149 (2nd)	Covered Hopper (twin)	29'3"	1,958	140,000	Greenville Steel Car Co.	1946	1989	106	---

1. Ribbed-side car bodies.
2. PM series 13525-13999 renumbered from G.E.T. (Government Equipment Trust) 36514-37027, 37400-37447.
3. Offset-side car bodies.

Flat Cars

NUMBERS	DESCRIPTION	LL	CU.FT.	LBS.	BUILDER	DATES	RETIRED	PAGE	NOTES
14000-14959 (1st)	Flat	33'0"-36'0"	---	40,000	F&PM	1881-1894	1921	---	---
15000-15019 (1st)	Flat	33'0"-34'0"	---	50,000		1881	1921	---	---
15020-15482 (1st)	Flat	34'0"	---	50,000	---	1881-1896	1922	---	---
15500-15599	Flat	36'0"	---	50,000	---	1881-1896	1921	---	---
16000-16267 (1st)	Flat	36'0"	---	60,000	---	1881-1896	1927	---	---
16268	Flat	36'0"	---	80,000	(Rebuilt) PM RR	1912	1927	---	---
16300-16399 (1st)	Flat	36'0"	---	60,000	---	1899	1927	---	1
16300-16319 (2nd)	Flat, steel underframe	40'8"	---	80,000	---	1943	1953	108	2
16400-16899 (1st)	Flat, steel underframe	37'0"	---	60,000	---	1899	1931	20	3
16900-16999	Flat	37'0"	---	60,000	Michigan-Peninsular Car Co.	18--	1927	---	---
16000-16099 (2nd)	Flat, steel	42'1"	---	100,000	Bethlehem Steel Co.	1930	1983	42	---
16500 (2nd)	Flat, steel underframe	40'10"	---	80,000	(Rebuilt) PM Ry.	1930	1941	44	4
16500-16749 (3rd)	Flat, steel	53'6"	---	140,000	Greenville Steel Car Co.	1942	1989	109	---
16750-16849 (2nd)	Flat, steel	53'6"	---	140,000	Greenville Steel Car Co.	1944	1991	109	5
18000	Flat	42'8"	---	80,000	---	---	1913	---	---

1. PM No. 16350 rebuilt to 100,000 pounds capacity by 1921.
2. Possibly rebuilt from box cars in PM series 89300-90349 in 1943.
3. The following cars were rebuilt by PM to 80,000 pounds capacity in 1912: 16431, 16629, 16643, 16678, 16680, 16696, 16809, 16829.
4. PM No. 16500 was converted from 40-ton box car No. 81279 (originally built by the McGuire Car Company in 1919 or 1920). This car was used between St. Louis, Michigan, and Saginaw, Michigan, and was equipped to carry water tanks owned by the Magnetic Springs Water Company of Saginaw.
5. C&O No. 216759 (ex-PM No. 16756) was the last surviving PM revenue freight car, lasting into 1991.

Box Cars

NUMBERS	DESCRIPTION	LL	CU.FT.	LBS.	BUILDER	DATES	RETIRED	PAGE	NOTES
500-699	Furniture, wood	40'0"	3,010	60,000	Haskell & Barker Car Co.	1892	1924	---	1
700-814	Furniture, wood	40'0"	3,010	60,000	American Car & Foundry Co.	1899	1923	---	---
900-949	Furniture, wood	38'0"	2,829	50,000	Wells & French	1891	1919	---	2
950-958	Furniture, wood	35'0"	---	50,000	---	1887	1920	---	---
960-985	Furniture, wood	40'8"	2,760	50,000	Wells & French	1891	1922	---	3
986-995	Furniture, wood	50'0"	3,780	60,000	Wells & French	1898	1921	---	---
996-998	Furniture, wood	45'0"	3,675	50,000	---	18--	1916	---	---
999	Furniture, wood	49'6"	3,726	50,000	---	18--	1916	---	---
1700-1799	Charcoal, wood	33'-35'	---	30,-40000	---	1899	1914	---	4
1800-1825	Charcoal, tight roof	33'-35'	---	30,-40000	---	1899	1914	---	4
2800-3016	Box, wood	27'-29'	---	24,-35000	---	18--	1916	---	5
3017-3149	Box, wood	27'-29'	---	24,-35000	---	18--	1916	---	5
3150-3479	Box, wood	32'-34'	---	40,000	---	18--	1916	---	---
3489-4999	Box, wood	32'-34'	---	30,-40000	---	1883-87	1916	---	---
5000-5383	Box, wood	32'-34'	---	30,-50000	---	1886	1920	---	6
5610-5633	Box, wood	33'0"	1,637	60,000	---	18--	1916	---	---
5635-5669	Box, wood	33'6"	1,810	60,000	---	18--	1916	---	---
5850-5858	Box, wood	37'5"	2,419	50,000	---	18--	1916	---	7
5870-5884	Box, wood	37'4"	2,562	50,000	---	18--	1916	---	---
5885-5999	Box, wood	37'4"	2,452	50,000	Muskegon Car Co.	1889	1919	---	---
6000-6249	Box, wood	35'10"	2,332	60,000	Michigan-Peninsular Car Co.	1898	1928	---	8
6300-6359	Box, wood	---	---	60,000	Muskegon Car Co.	1892	1929	---	---
6360-6592	Box, wood	---	---	60,000	Muskegon Car Co.	1899	1929	---	---
6600-6923	Box, wood	38'0"	2,459	60,000	---	1898	1929	---	---
6924-6946	Box, wood	---	---	60,000	Muskegon Car Co.	1899	1929	---	---
6989-6999	Box, wood	34'0"	1,950	60,000	Muskegon Car Co.	1899	1916	---	---
7000-7155	Box, wood (ventilated)	38'0"	2,429	60,000	Michigan-Peninsular Car Co.	1890	1928	---	---
7200-7207	Box, wood (ventilated)	36'0"	2,448	60,000	---	18--	1928	20	---
7500-7999	Box, wood	38'0"	2,429	60,000	American Car & Foundry Co.	1900	1929	21	---
8000-8499	Box, wood	38'0"	2,429	60,000	American Car & Foundry Co.	1901	1929	---	---
20000-21999 (1st)	Box, wood	33'0"	---	---	---	18--	1907	---	---
20025-20305 (2nd)	Automobile, wood	36'0"	2,448	60,000	---	---	1929	---	9
22000-22999	Box, wood	33'9"	---	30,000	---	18--	1908	---	---
26000-26999	Box, wood	33'9"	---	50,000	---	18--	1908	---	---
28000-28049	Box, wood	36'2"	---	60,000	---	18--	1912	---	---
30000-30508	Box, wood	36'0"	2,448	60,000	American Car & Foundry Co.	1902	1913	22	10, 11
30509-30527	Box, wood	36'0"	2,448	60,000	Haskell & Barker Car Co.	1904	1930	---	10, 11
31000-31999	Box, wood	36'0"	2,448	60,000	Haskell & Barker Car Co.	1904	1930	---	10, 11
32000-33249	Box, wood	36'0"	2,424	60,000	American Car & Foundry Co.	1905	1930	23	10, 11
40000-42649	Box, wood	38'0"	2,136	60,000	American Car & Foundry Co.	1903	1934	24	10, 11

Box Cars (continued)

NUMBERS	DESCRIPTION	LL	CU.FT.	LBS.	BUILDER	DATES	RETIRED	PAGE	NOTES
42650-43149	Vehicle, wood	36'0"	2,524	60,000	American Car & Foundry Co.	1903	1934	28	10, 11, 12
43150-43649	Box, wood	38'0"	2,136	60,000	American Car & Foundry Co.	1903	1934	24	10, 11
50000-52499	Box, wood	36'0"	2,524	80,000	The Pullman Company	1906-1909	1934	30	11
52500-52999	Automobile, wood	36'0"	2,524	80,000	The Pullman Company	1906-1909	1934	30	11
53000-53999	Box, wood	36'0"	2,524	80,000	The Pullman Company	1906-1909	1934	30	11
54000-54051	Auto, steel underframe	40'6"	3,170	75,000	Western Steel Car & Foundry	1922-1923	1953	64/70	13, 14
54055-54059	Auto, steel underframe	40'6"	3,712	70,000	Pressed Steel Car Co.	1929	1957	78	18, 20
54100-54163	Auto, steel underframe	40'6"	3,170	80,000	Pressed Steel Car Co.	1922-1923	1954	64/70	13, 15
54200-54244	Auto, steel underframe	40'6"	3,170	80,000	Western Steel Car & Foundry	1922-1923	1954	64/70	13, 16
54225-54239	Box, steel underframe	40'6"	3,170	80,000	Western Steel Car & Foundry	1922-1923	1953	64/70	13, 16
54240	Auto, steel underframe	40'6"	3,170	80,000	Western Steel Car & Foundry	1922-1923	1951	64/70	13, 16, 20
54250-54254	Box, steel underframe	40'6"	3,712	80,000	Pressed Steel Car Co.	1929	1955	78	18, 20
54260-54274	Box, steel underframe	40'6"	3,712	80,000	Pressed Steel Car Co.	1929	1957	78	18, 20
54600-54344	Auto, steel underframe	40'6"	3,403	70,000	Pressed Steel Car Co.	1927	1955	74	17
54345-54348	Auto, steel underframe	40'6"	3,403	70,000	Pressed Steel Car Co.	1927	1957	74	17, 20
54500-54548	Auto, steel underframe	40'6"	3,170	75,000	Western Steel Car & Foundry	1922-1923	1953	64/70	13
54550	Auto, steel underframe	40'6"	3,712	75,000	Pressed Steel Car Co.	1929	1951	78	18
54570-54571	Auto, steel underframe	40'6"	3,170	75,000	Western Steel Car & Foundry	1922-1923	1953	64/70	13, 20
54600-54620	Auto, steel underframe	40'6"	3,403	80,000	Pressed Steel Car Co.	1927	1960	74	17
54700-54709	Auto, steel underframe	40'6"	3,712	80,000	Pressed Steel Car Co.	1929	1960	78	18
54800-54835	Box, steel underframe	40'6"	3,712	80,000	Pressed Steel Car Co.	1929	1958	78	18, 20
55001	Box, steel underframe	40'6"	3,170	80,000	Western Steel Car & Foundry	1922-1923	1945	64	13
55100	Auto, steel underframe	40'6"	3,403	80,000	Pressed Steel Car Co.	1927	1959	74	17
55200-55209	Auto, steel underframe	40'6"	3,712	80,000	Pressed Steel Car Co.	1929	1960	78	18, 19
55300-55309	Auto, steel underframe	40'6"	3,170	80,000	Western Steel Car & Foundry	1922-1923	1953	65/70	13, 21
55310-55319	Box, steel underframe	40'6"	3,170	80,000	Western Steel Car & Foundry	1922-1923	1953	64/70	13
55400-55407	Auto, steel underframe	40'6"	3,170	80,000	Western Steel Car & Foundry	1922-1923	1954	64/70	13
55500-55527	Box, steel underframe	40'6"	3,712	80,000	Pressed Steel Car Co.	1929	1954	78	18
55600-55694	Auto, steel underframe	40'6"	3,712	80,000	Pressed Steel Car Co.	1929	1967	78	18, 20
55750-55799	Auto, steel underframe	40'6"	3,712	80,000	Pressed Steel Car Co.	1929	1967	78	18, 20
56000-56014	Auto, steel underframe	40'6"	3,712	80,000	Pressed Steel Car Co.	1929	1955	78	18
56100-56199	Auto, steel underframe	40'6"	3,712	80,000	Pressed Steel Car Co.	1929	1947	78	18
56300-56316	Auto, steel underframe	40'6"	3,712	65,000	Pressed Steel Car Co.	1929	1954	78	18, 20, 22
59500-59529	Auto, steel	50'6"	4,545	75,000	Pressed Steel Car Co.	1930	1960	83	23
59600-59611	Auto, steel	50'6"	4,545	70,000	Pressed Steel Car Co.	1930	1965	83	23
59700-59727	Auto, steel	50'6"	4,545	65,000	Pressed Steel Car Co.	1930	1965	83	23, 36
59728	Box, steel	50'6"	4,545	75,000	Pressed Steel Car Co.	1930	1954	83	23
54750-59763	Box, steel	50'6"	4,545	75,000	Ralston Steel Car Co.	1936	1957	86	24
60001-60014	Auto, steel underframe	40'6"	3,403	70,000	Pressed Steel Car Co.	1927	1955	73	17, 25
60015-60019	Box, steel underframe	40'6"	3,403	80,000	Pressed Steel Car Co.	1927	1957	73	17, 25
60050-60064	Auto, steel underframe	40'6"	3,712	75,000	Pressed Steel Car Co.	1929	1955	78	18

Box Cars (continued)

NUMBERS	DESCRIPTION	LL	CU.FT.	LBS.	BUILDER	DATES	RETIRED	PAGE	NOTES
60060-60064	Box, steel underframe	40'6"	3,712	80,000	Pressed Steel Car Co.	1929	1955	78	18, 20
61001-61040	Box, steel underframe	40'6"	3,098	80,000	Standard Steel Car Co.	1920	1946	59	26
61041-61050	Box, steel underframe	40'6"	3,098	80,000	Pacific Car & Foundry Co.	1920	1945	59	26, 27
62001-62015	Box, steel underframe	40'6"	3,098	80,000	(Various)	1919-1920	1939	59	26, 27
63001-63060	Box, steel underframe	40'6"	3,403	80,000	Pressed Steel Car Co.	1927	1957	74	17, 28
64001-64050	Box, steel underframe	40'6"	3,098	80,000	(Various)	1919-1920	1946	59	26, 29
64075-64084	Auto, steel underframe	40'6"	3,712	80,000	Pressed Steel Car Co.	1929	1942	78	18
65001-65061	Box, steel underframe	40'6"	3,712	80,000	Pressed Steel Car Co.	1929	1965	78	18, 30
65062-65069	Box, steel underframe	40'6"	3,712	80,000	Pressed Steel Car Co.	1929	1955	78	18, 30
65070-65093	Box, steel underframe	40'6"	3,712	80,000	Pressed Steel Car Co.	1929	1947	78	18, 30
67050-67057	Box, steel underframe	40'6"	3,098	80,000	(Various)	1919-1920	1946	59	26, 31
68001-68049	Auto, steel underframe	40'6"	3,712	80,000	Pressed Steel Car Co.	1929	1942	78	18, 32
68050-68069	Auto, steel underframe	40'6"	3,712	75,000	Pressed Steel Car Co.	1929	1942	78	18
69045-69054	Auto, steel underframe	40'6"	3,098	80,000	Standard Steel Car Co.	1920	1946	59	33
69055-69099	Auto, steel underframe	40'6"	3,098	80,000	(Various)	1919-1920	1946	59	15, 26
70000-70999	Box, steel center sill	40'6"	3,098	80,000	Haskell & Barker Car Co.	1917-1918	1943	57	39
71000-71249	Furniture, steel	50'6"	4,545	75,000	Pressed Steel Car Co.	1930	1974	83	34, 35, 36
71250-71349	Auto, steel	50'6"	4,587	65,000	Ralston Steel Car Co.	1936	1976	86	35, 36
72000-72049	Auto, steel	50'6"	4,629	100,000	Greenville Steel Car Co.	1940	1976	126	37, 38
72050-72099	Auto-furniture, steel	50'6"	4,629	100,000	Greenville Steel Car Co.	1940	1984	126	38
72100-75124	Auto-furniture, steel	50'6"	4,629	100,000	Greenville Steel Car Co.	1941	1985	129	38
72125-72149	Auto-furniture, steel	50'6"	4,629	100,000	Greenville Steel Car Co.	1941	1976	130	34, 38
72150-72199	Auto, steel	50'6"	4,629	100,000	Greenville Steel Car Co.	1941	1976	130	34, 38
72200-72349	Auto, steel	50'6"	4,871	100,000	Ralston Steel Car Co.	1946	1985	132	---
72350-72399	Damage-free box, steel	50'6"	4,837	100,000	Ralston Steel Car Co.	1946	1985	132	37
80000-80499	Auto, steel u.f. (USRA)	40'6"	3,098	80,000	Standard Steel Car Co.	1920	1945	61	39
80500-80999	Box, steel u.f. (USRA)	40'6"	3,098	80,000	Standard Steel Car Co.	1920	1945	62	---
81000-81109	Box, steel u.f. (USRA)	40'6"	3,098	80,000	Keith Car & Manufacturing Co.	1919	1945	62	---
81110-81323	Box, steel u.f. (USRA)	40'6"	3,098	80,000	McGuire Car Co.	1920	1945	62	40
81324-81999	Box, steel u.f. (USRA)	40'6"	3,098	80,000	Pacific Car & Foundry Co.	1920	1945	62	---
82000-83499	Box, steel	40'6"	3,053	100,000	Standard Steel Car. Co.	1930	1983	81	---
83500-83649	Box, steel	40'6"	3,712	100,000	American Car & Foundry Co.	1941	1984	115	---
83650-83799	Box, steel	40'6"	3,712	100,000	Pullman-Standard Car Mfg. Co.	1940-1941	1976	119	---
83800-83999	Box, steel	40'6"	3,712	100,000	General American Trans. Corp.	1941	1984	115	---
84000-84099	Box, lightweight steel (welded)	40'6"	3,733	100,000	Pullman-Standard Car Mfg. Co.	1940	1977	120	---
84100-84199	Box, steel	40'6"	3,712	100,000	American Car & Foundry Co.	1941	1975	122	---
84200-84299	Box, steel	40'6"	3,712	100,000	General American Trans. Corp.	1941	1978	122	---
84300-84399	Box, steel	40'6"	3,712	100,000	Pullman-Standard Car Mfg. Co.	1941	1975	122	---
85000-85999	Box, steel underframe	40'6"	3,170	80,000	Western Steel Car & Foundry	1922-1923	1957	63	41
86000-87499	Box, steel underframe	40'6"	3,170	80,000	Pressed Steel Car Co.	1923	1957	67	---
88000-88349	Box, steel underframe	40'6"	3,403	80,000	National Steel Car Co.	1927	1957	71	36, 42

Box Cars (continued)

NUMBERS	DESCRIPTION	LL	CU.FT.	LBS.	BUILDER	DATES	RETIRED	PAGE	NOTES
88350-89299	Box, steel underframe	40'6"	3,403	80,000	Pressed Steel Car Co.	1927	1958	73	---
89300-89349	Box, steel underframe	40'6"	3,712	80,000	Pressed Steel Car Co.	1927	1934	73	43
89350-90349	Box, steel underframe	40'6"	3,712	80,000	Pressed Steel Car Co.	1929	1983	77	41
90350-90399	Box, steel	40'6"	3,712	80,000	Pullman Car & Mfg Co.	1930	1975	89	---
90400-90499	Box, steel	40'6"	3,712	80,000	Pullman Car & Mfg Co.	1930	1970	89	44
90500-90849	Box, steel	40'6"	3,712	80,000	Pullman Car & Mfg Co.	1930	1978	89	---
90850-90999	Box, steel	40'6"	3,712	80,000	Pullman Car & Mfg Co.	1930	1975	89	45
91000-91499	Box, steel	40'6"	3,712	80,000	Pullman Car & Mfg Co.	1930	1975	89	45
91500-91699	Box, steel	40'6"	3,712	80,000	Pullman Car & Mfg Co.	1930	1974	89	45
91700-91849	Box, steel	40'6"	3,712	80,000	Pullman Car & Mfg Co.	1930	1975	89	45
91850-92349	Box, steel	40'6"	3,712	80,000	Pressed Steel Car Co.	1930	1974	89	34
93000-93199	Auto, steel	40'6"	3,847	80,000	Ralston Steel Car Co.	1936	1975	93	45
93200-93399	Auto, steel	40'6"	3,847	80,000	Ralston Steel Car Co.	1936	1973	93	45
93400-93499	Auto, steel	40'6"	3,847	80,000	Ralston Steel Car Co.	1941	1974	138	45

1. Renumbered from C&WM series 10000-10398 (even numbers only).
2. Renumbered from C&WM series 1986-2086 (even numbers only).
3. Renumbered from F&PM series 6700-6729.
4. Renumbered from F&PM series 1900-1999 and 6050-6058.
5. Renumbered from F&PM series 1-499.
6. Renumbered from F&PM series 6500-6699.
7. Renumbered from F&PM series 2810-2834.
8. Renumbered from F&PM series 500-799.
9. Eleven cars in series, acquired 1919-1920; possibly renumbered from PM series 30000-30508.
10. Equipped with small lumber doors in one end.
11 By 1931, a number of cars in this series were rebuilt with staggered double-doors.
12. By 1908, 25 cars in this series were equipped with full-sized end doors; by 1911, 48 cars were so equipped.
13. Cars in this series were renumbered from PM series 85000-85999 and/or 86000-87499.
14. Originally equipped for handling automotive steering gears.
15. Equipped for handling Chevrolet castings.
16 Equipped for handling Chevrolet bumpers.
17. Cars in this series were renumbered from PM series 88350-89299.
18. Cars in this series were renumbered from PM series 89350-90349.
19. Equipped for handling miscellaneous seating equipment other than automobile seats.
20. Renumbered after C&O merger in 1947, but lettered PM.
21. Equipped for handling gas-oil furnaces.
22. Equipped for handling refrigeration compressor units.

23. Cars in this series renumbered from PM series 71000-71249.
24. Cars in this series renumbered from PM series 71250-71349.
25. Equipped for handling Buick transmissions.
26. Cars in this series renumbered from PM series 80500-81999 when rebuilt.
27. Equipped for handling Buick motors and gas tanks.
28. Equipped for handling Chevrolet transmissions.
29. Equipped for handling Buick axles.
30. Equipped for handling Ford hubs.
31. Equipped for handling Kelsey-Hayes castings.
32. Equipped for handling auto bodies.
33. Cars in this series renumbered from PM series 80000-80499.
34. Equipped with end doors.
35. Some cars in this series equipped with special loading devices and perforated linings.
36. Some cars had auxiliary doors permanently closed.
37. Equipped with perforated steel lining; auxiliary doors permanently closed.
38. Equipped with Duryea cushion underframes.
39. Originally single-door cars; rebuilt with staggered double-doors.
40. PM No. 81279 converted to flat car No. 16500 (2nd), 1930.
41. Auxiliary doors removed.
42. These cars were built in Canada and were at home on PM lines in Ontario.
43. Cars in PM series 89300-89349 converted to single-deck stock cars (PM 2000-2049 [2nd]), in 1934.
44. Cars leased to Chesapeake & Ohio Railway in May 1935; renumbered to C&O series 6600-6699.
45. Equipped by PM with Evans auto loaders.

Pere Marquette steel box car No. 83348 was photographed in August 1940, shortly after being reweighed at the Saginaw, Michigan, shops (SAG 5-40). Built by Standard Steel Car Company in 1930, it was part of 1,500 cars in series 82000-83499. Nearly identical C&O and Erie cars used Climax radial roofs, but the PM cars had Hutchins roofs. Apex metal running boards were applied to 363 of the cars in 1943-45. Many of the cars lasted into the C&O era, and were upgraded with AB brakes. More than 75 cars were assigned to auto parts service in 1949-50.

PERE
MARQUETTE

PERE
MARQUETTE

Appendix B

Pere Marquette
Lettering Diagrams

Hopper Cars 13000-14499

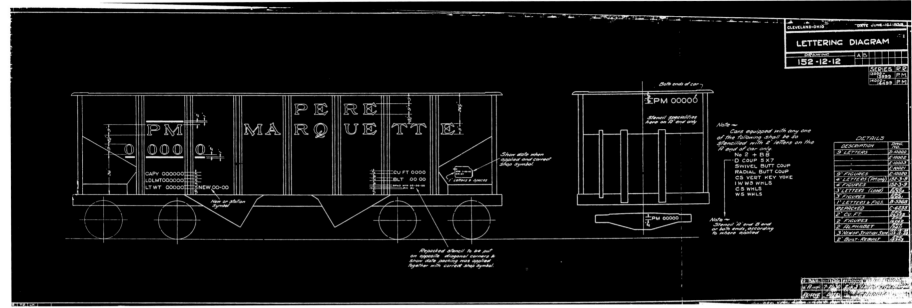

Hopper Cars 15000-15249

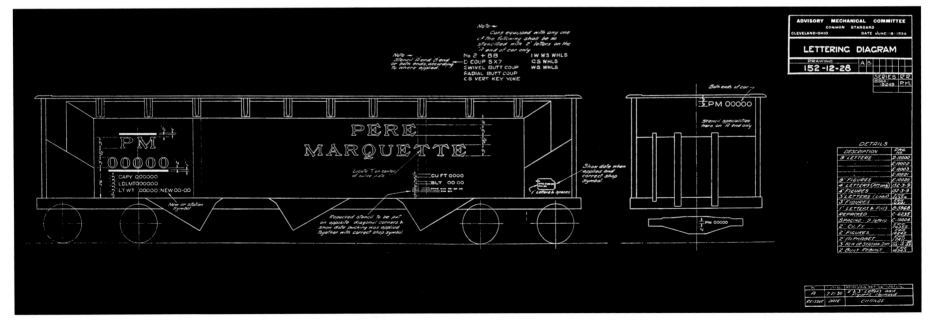

Flat Cars 16000-16099

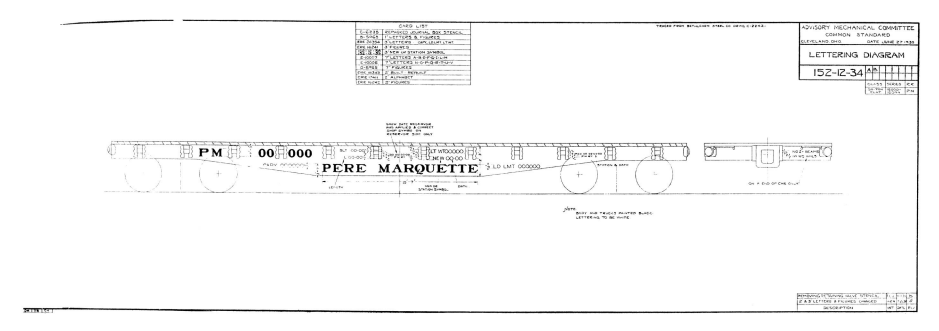

Flat Cars 16750-16849

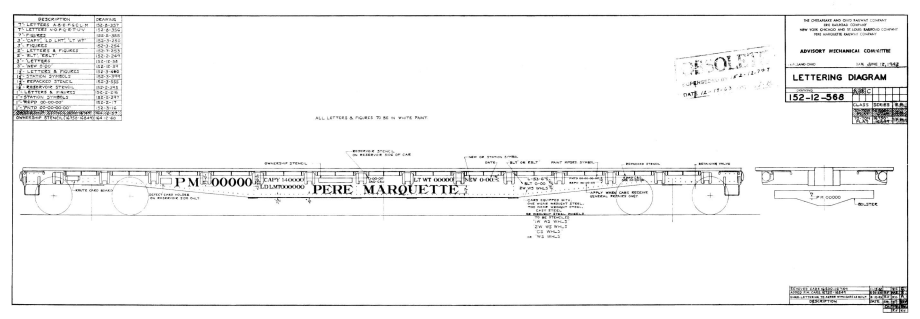

Gondola Cars 17000-17649

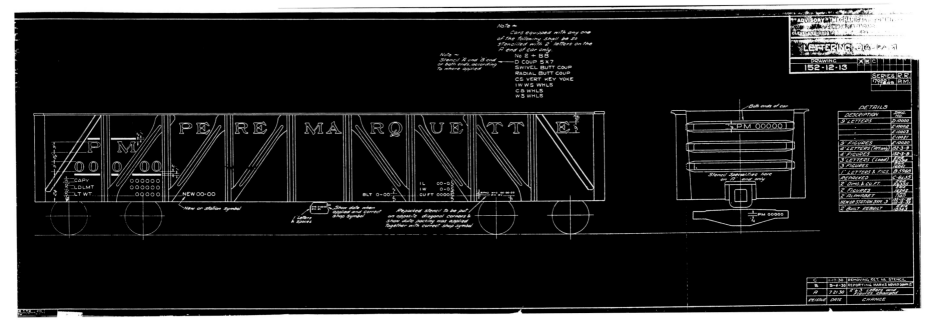

Gondola Cars 17650-18399

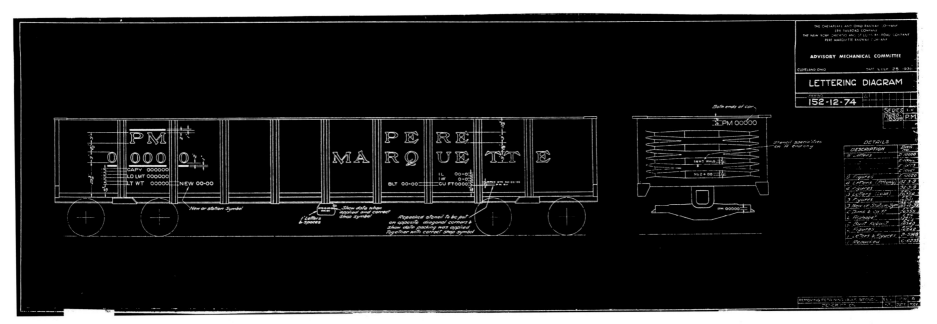

Gondola Cars 18400-18649

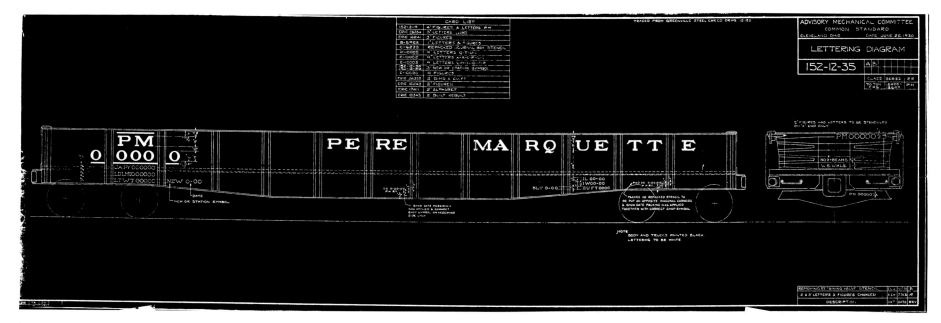

Gondola Cars 18850-18949

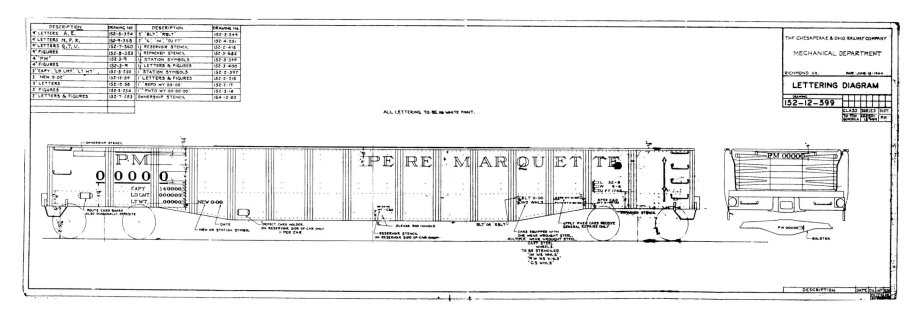

Refrigerator Cars 25000-25299

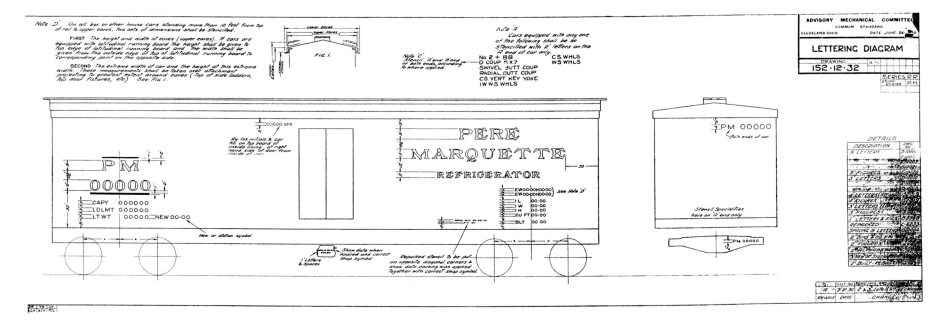

Box Cars 84100-84399

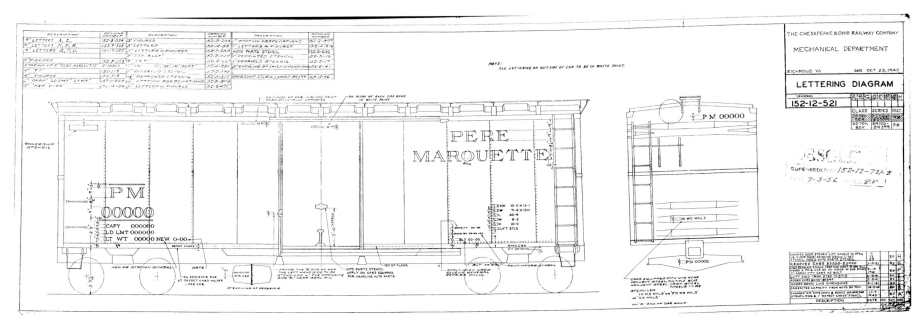

50' Auto Cars 72100-72199

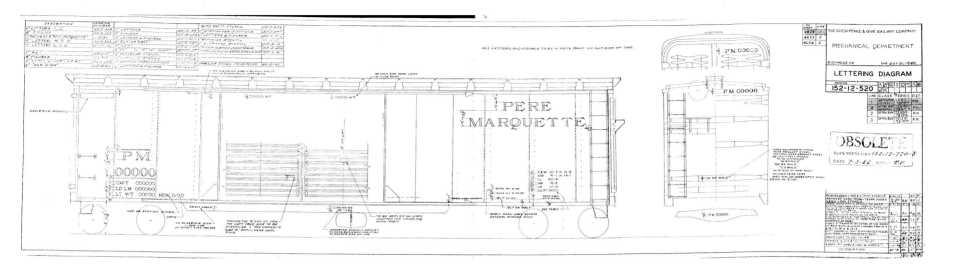

50' Auto Cars 72200-72399

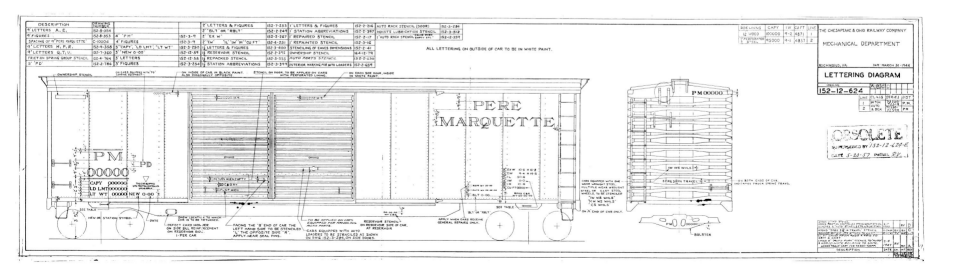

Box Cars 85000-89299

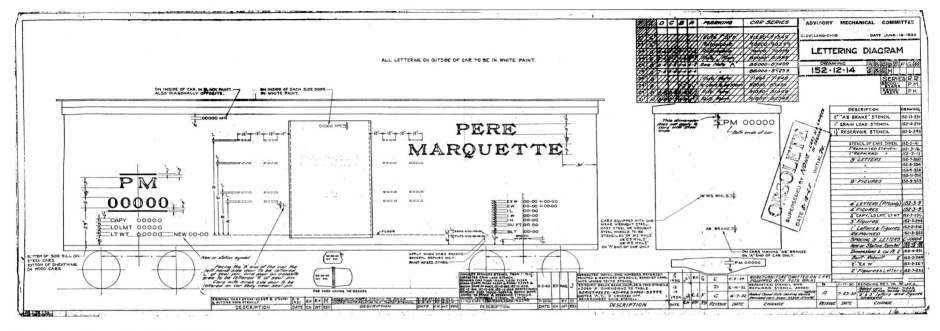

40' Auto Cars 93400-93499

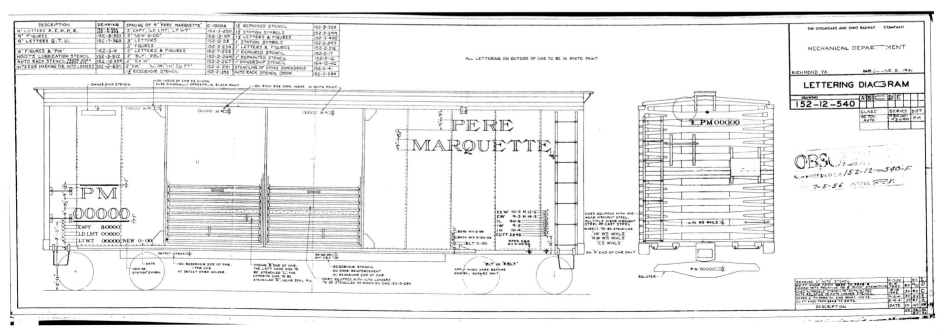